HOLLYWOOD'S GOLDEN AGE

As Told By One Who Lived It All

HOLLYWOOD'S GOLDEN AGE

As Told By One Who Lived It All

Edward Dmytryk

BearManor Media
2003

Hollywood's Golden Age: As Told By One Who Lived It All

For information, address:

BearManor Media
P. O. Box 750
Boalsburg, PA 16827

bearmanormedia.com

Cover design by John Teehan
Typesetting and layout by John Teehan

Published in the USA by BearManor Media
ISBN - 0-9714570-4-2
Library of Congress Control No. 2003100757

HOLLYWOOD'S GOLDEN AGE

As Told By One Who Lived It All

Edward Dmytryk

While the photos contained in this book do not exactly fit the context of the text, they do represent an assemblage of Dmytryk's life and work, and compliment the memories that make up the man. All photos are from the Dmytryk family collection.

FOREWORD

For many people their work is the most important thing in life and my husband was one of those. Making motion pictures filled his heart and his mind; it was a very good heart and a fabulous mind. I'm grateful to have shared that exciting life with him for fifty-three years. Oh yes, there were times when I knew I was in the back seat, even when he was whispering "I love you more than anything in the world"…sure, sure …but I stood my ground and kept my place, for in the long run, I loved his work as much as he did. He was a master and a major player.

Edward was sixteen years old when he discovered how filmed stories were made, and he maintained throughout his lifetime that CUTTING was the art of it all. He started in the mail room at Famous-Lasky Paramount Studio, progressed to assistant projectionist and was soon their most preferred projectionist called upon to run special showings and previews, where he learned from watching everything that was shown including foreign masterpieces.

While delivering film back and forth to the cutting department, he found himself spending more and more time watching and learning the editing process. This is where it was made…rough or smooth, good or bad…this was the finished product. He made up his mind he wanted to be a cutter.

But, at this very same time he was offered a scholarship at Caltech, one of the most prestigious universities in the United States. He didn't know what to do and asked for advice from knowledgeable and respected friends and the consensus was, "Grab it!" So he did.

While grinding away at math, biology and physics, he found he had left his heart on Marathon Street in Hollywood. What??!! With Jean Harlow?! He had been bitten by the magic of movies. Having kept his foot in the door to the studio by working holidays and weekends, at the end of the school year he returned and the studio was glad to have him back.

He requested the cutting department and was given a job as an assistant to Roy Stone, one of the top editors in the business. Eddie's life at this point was such that he could devote any and all time to his craft. Soon, he was a full cutter and found that all of the tedious hours of scientific study would not be wasted. He found use for all of those skills in his cutting and timing, so much so that the most important directors, George Cukor and Leo McCarey, asked that Eddie be "on the set" to advise them on camera set-ups, saving hours of time and reams of film.

From all this, proving that his knowledge and experience were invaluable, he was given a chance to direct. Of course that's what he wanted, but on the first day he set foot on the sound stage as being in charge, he was scared to death.

These were "B" movies at first, of course, low budgets, allowing the directors to try things without worrying if they would break the bank. He never went beyond the schedule or over budget, and he never shot anything he wouldn't use. He made many "B"s over a couple of years and in 1943, RKO gave him a small film that became a sleeper. It broke all kinds of box office records and took RKO out of the red. The title of the movie was *Hitler's Children* and Eddie was given the title of "Mr. RKO." And, he was given a new contract.

Along with all this excitement, he once again had the heebie-jeebies when he realized his next assignment was to be a big budget "A" film, starring one of RKO's big names, Ginger Rogers. On their first day of working together, he braced himself as he faced the star, but she put him totally at ease and he wondered if she knew how he felt. They got along beautifully together and all nerves were put to rest. But he never forgot the huge sums of money for which he would be held accountable.

Two films that he was particularly proud of during those years, were *Murder, My Sweet*, which gave him the opportunity to use some clever special effects he personally dreamed up, and *Crossfire*, a very different kind of "hate crime." Both were big box office hits. In fact, *Crossfire* was nominated that year for Best Film (1947). Eddie shot that film in 21 days at a cost of

Jean and Eddie Dmytryk, 1952.

$250,000. It made millions for the studio and brought in many awards.

Eddie went on to make thirty more films, big and small, some of them award-winning (*The Caine Mutiny* with Humphrey Bogart, *The Young Lions* with Marlon Brando and Montgomery Clift, *Broken Lance* with Spencer Tracy) and all of the others were good. We traveled all over the world on locations, widening our understanding of peoples everywhere, and Eddie started writing.

Eddie's experiences, good and bad, in all areas, were the product of his curiosity and his need for knowledge.

He was a great man, sensitive and complex, but great.

– JEAN PORTER DMYTRYK
March 2003

CHAPTER ONE

She was just one month and twelve days short of her twelfth birthday on the day I was born. However, I didn't meet her until 1923, when I was fourteen-and-a-half and she was twenty-six. To tell the truth, I wasn't formally introduced, but we did talk. I think she said, "Thank you," and I said, "You're welcome, Miss Gish."

I had been working at Famous Players-Lasky studio for about eight weeks; not nearly long enough to be glutted with glamour, and in my short life Lillian Gish was unquestionably the most beautiful woman I had ever seen in the flesh. "In the flesh" is an improper phrase, but it will do as a contrast to frame the reality: she was elegant, cool, immaculately dressed in summer white from dainty shoes to soft, broad-brimmed hat. Ethereal—that's the word. It was probably that quality, a quality she retained throughout her life, that kept me from acquiring an instant crush—she was a woman to regard with awe, not to fall in love with.

Except for Katharine Hepburn, no star of today can be looked at in the same way, but in the early days of filmmaking such women existed and such things did happen. Here I was, a homeless fourteen-year-old, working my way through high school as a 'gofer' at the dilapidated remnants of the Famous Players-Lasky editing and projection room complex on Argyle Avenue just south of Selma which, as the crow flies, is a block-and-a-half from Hollywood and Vine. And I had just been summoned to Victor Clark's office, a short walk across the lot near the main studio entrance on Vine Street.

Victor Clark is one of Hollywood's many forgotten names, but in 1923 he was co-chief of the studio. It was through his good graces, at the intercession of

5

Harry James, the founder of a boys' organization I had belonged to, that I was working after school and on Saturdays for six dollars a week. Much later I came to realize the job was created for me as an act of charity and a favor to a friend. There have been more notable acts of largesse, to be sure, for even then six bucks a week could hardly bankrupt a growing business, but it did afford me the rental of a sleeping porch I called home, and for that I was grateful.

Clark's executive partner was Charles Eyton, a warm and amiable man, which means that even in the Hollywood of 1923 he was an anomaly. But what distinguished him even more was that he also worked 'in the ring' as a referee for the four-round fights promoted weekly in the suburb of Vernon by Leo McCarey's father. (Four rounds was then the legal limit for all bouts in California.) Eyton was lucky to have this 'moonlight' job since both he and Clark were soon to become anonymous. In the next few years Famous Players Lasky adopted the name of its releasing company and Paramount Pictures was born.

To repeat, I had been called to Clark's office and found him bidding Miss Gish a good afternoon. I was handed a very long flower box (American Beauties?) to take to her car. (In 1923 no 'lady' carried her packages, and every store with any claim to quality hired young boys to do the carrying for them. Child labor laws were realistic then, and many boys from the age of twelve up used their spare time to augment the family funds. At least it can be said that to a considerable extent poor kids were kept off the streets and out of gangs; they also learned the work ethic and slid from school to treadmill or career without fear or panic.)

Miss Gish's limousine and driver were waiting on Vine Street, one of Hollywood's highroads, which served to ratify the judgment of those who still called Hollywood a village. Only the two central lanes were paved, with a tar which, before macadam came into general use, bubbled during the occasional Southern California heat waves, and which we kids used to gouge out and chew in place of gum. The outside, or curb lanes, were made of steamrollered decomposed granite which the surrounding semi-arid country supplied in plenty, and gravel (ditto). Enhancing the sense of pleasant countrification, large, gracefully pendulous California Pepper trees (borrowed from South America) shaded both sides of the street. Unfortunately, the California Pepper, for many years a great favorite, is a 'dirty' tree, which sheds its leaves and 'berries' throughout the year. It is now rarely seen in the area.

Intersecting Vine Street a half-block south of the studio's main entrance, Sunset Boulevard effectively divided Hollywood into the rich and the not so rich. It was the community's "Apian Way," the longest street in the state, some said in the world. From its humble beginnings at the Plaza in L.A.'s historic downtown center, it wound its way through the western part of the city and a number of its suburbs, including Hollywood and Beverly Hills, until it met the Pacific Ocean near Inceville, the Thomas Ince studio just northwest of Santa Monica. The stretch bisecting Hollywood was distinguished by its closely planted palm trees, interspaced with bright red flowering rose bushes. Ah! Sweet nostalgia.

Still under the spell of this movie legend, my eyes followed Miss Gish's limousine as it turned west on the boulevard. In later years I met, knew, and worked with a host of "legends," but time and familiarity eroded my sense of wonder, and only one other person recreated that instantaneous impression made on me by Miss Gish. But this one was meant to be loved.

Finally I came back to earth and my eyes were drawn to Joe Oblath's lunch wagon, permanently parked at the edge of an empty lot just across the street. I was tempted to run over to buy a drink, but Cokes cost a nickel and I didn't have that much money to throw around. I decided to return to my post on the seedy side of the lot.

Joe Oblath and his sons were as intimately connected with Paramount as any of those within its gates. Some time in the mid '20s the studio established its presence on Marathon Avenue, next door to FBO (later RKO). Joe realized that if Zukor and Lasky could move to roomier quarters, so could he; he was not about to lose his clientele. He abandoned his Vine Street luncheonette, leased (or bought) the southwest corner of Marathon and Bronson Avenues, just opposite the studio's auto gate, and continued to serve breakfast, lunch and late-night dinners to thousands of craftsmen, extras, actors, and stars, until the late '80s. Before his sons took over, Joe had outlasted dozens of Paramount's presidents, vice-presidents, and stars. I have always thought of Paramount as my mother and father, but Joe was everybody's uncle and occasional best friend. He carried the tabs of nearly as many hard-pressed actors as did the Schwabs at their drug store on Sunset Boulevard—but that's another story.

For years Oblath's featured one counter and a single line of seven or eight booths; these were later augmented by a few tables in a rather murky side room. The tableware consisted of the ubiquitous coffee mugs, cheap plates, bowls, and eating utensils, but Joe kept a small hoard of delicate china, which was brought out only for special customers (mostly writers) on very special occasions—election days. After the Volstead Act died liquor sales were illegal until the polls had closed, which made it hard on artists who needed stimulation. At Oblath's one could have "tea" and inspiration in fine china cups at any hour of the day.

My memories of Paramount in the '30s are highlighted by the presence of two men, one of whom, Jack Oakie, was as much an Oblath feature as the china cups. On his days off, which, given the schedule of the average production, were many, Jack could be found in an Oblath booth or out on the corner looking for an invitation to slide into one. Artists are generally believed to be profligate, but a small number of top actors have been known to squeeze a nickel until the Indian (later, Thomas Jefferson) begged for mercy. Jack had the grip of a wrestler. His usual targets were projectionists, editors, and their assistants, and at one time or another I have been all of these. For the price of a cup of coffee and a doughnut or Danish, we would enjoy the latest jokes and comic comments on current issues delivered by an artist. We considered him a companion who had strayed. He met us on dead level ground, which we appreciated, and there was not an ounce of pretension or arrogance in Oakie's rather plump body. More than any comedian he established the "second banana" as nearly indispensable in Hollywood films, and he invented that greatest of all comedy "shtick," the triple take. When properly executed it has never failed to get a proper laugh.

George M. Cohan was of a different breed. The panhandlers on Oblath's corner were always on their toes when he was in the studio, and he never failed them. To the workers on the set he seemed distant and aloof, but he never slighted a moocher. He kept the precept, "There but for the grace of God, go I," forever in his mind and a supply of silver dollars in his pocket. During the Great Depression a blue-plate special cost thirty-five cents, and one dollar could keep a man alive for some time.

I crossed the stages on my way back to what we called the "old lab"—a "new" lab was already under construction on the west side of Argyle Avenue. Almost everyone now active in filmmaking will be puzzled by my use of the word "crossed," but yes, at Famous Players it was not only possible, but quite necessary, to "cross" the stage rather than "walk through it." Of the studio's four stages only one had walls, a ceiling, and a roof. Stages 1, 2, and 3, were simply extensive platforms. Made of rough, stout lumber and raised two or three feet above the bare soil, each was some 150 to 200 feet long and about 75 feet wide. Placed side-by-side they covered about an acre of ground. The reason for such structures was simple: incandescent lighting had not yet been perfected and "Klieg lights," though used for night lighting, were too harsh for most actors of the day. The sun was still the most available and certainly the cheapest source of light for exposing film. Even stage 4, the only enclosed stage on the lot, had glass sides and a glass roof to "let the sun shine in."

The studio was busy, and rarely was a stage occupied by just one company, which has been the established practice since the advent of sound. On one of my frequent trips of discovery I hit a bonanza: on stage 2, three companies were shooting on the same day. The property man from one of the crews apparently mistook me for Jesse Lasky, Jr., or Victor Clark's son, both of whom were my age. He hustled a director's chair so I could watch the action in comfort and enjoy my panoramic view of three companies for the price of one. I would never again stumble onto such a bargain.

Looking like railroad flats with their front walls removed, the sets for three films had been lined up side-by-side by art directors who were probably unaware they might be used simultaneously. But the odds had been beaten and here they were: three directors, three casts of actors, and three crews, all going at it without regard to interference from offstage noises or onstage voices. Each crew had its own background "orchestra," usually just a harmonium, but often accompanied by a violin or an accordion. When the director on one of the sets called "Action!" the air would be suffused with melodies best suited to the mood of the scene. But when the action on all three sets occasionally coincided, all hell broke loose. The mixture of three tunes (usually in three different keys) combined with the voices of three directors soothing or spurring the actors on through their megaphones created a cacophony unrivalled in the world of music until the onset of "heavy metal." Thank God none of this frantic devil's chorus ever hit the screen, yet it was the one time I enjoyed such a noise, and was not displeased at being taken for a rich man's son.

However, too much was soon quite enough. I thanked the prop man for his courtesy and wandered down to the southwest corner of the lot where, squeezed between stages 3 and 4, the building used by Apfel and DeMille as a stage for the making of *The Squaw Man* had been mothballed for the duration. I found it of little interest. However, I was always interested in the "human genre," and on the northwest corner of stage 1 I stopped at the spot where Wally Reid and his little jazz band, made up of set musicians and studio hands, had spent their lunch hours in harmonic escape from the pressures of manufacturing entertainment for the masses.

Wallace Reid was perhaps the first of Hollywood's tragic figures. He was a handsome, athletic man with an interest in sports and music. Until 1922 he was one of the most important of Lasky's Famous Players. But in 1919 he had suffered severe head injuries in a train crash and was given frequent doses of morphine to ease the pain. The pain ceased in time, but the morphine refused to surrender its advantage; Reid became addicted, not only to the drug but also to alcohol. He died in 1923 at the age of 32, the first of a long line of film artists to follow that particular road to deliverance from pain, not all of which was physical.

I was too young, too inexperienced to understand that fame and status rarely paved the way to total satisfaction, or that an honest pursuit of art often bagged more hurt than happiness. I just sat there, staring at a patch of bare flooring where only a few months ago fulfilling music had been played, feeling sorrow for the man who had been fated to face death in such an inelegant fashion.

But I had little time for extended rumination. In my first few weeks on the job my workload was light, but when some slight matter needed my inexpert attention my boss, Claude Baldridge, expected to find me at my post.

On my way back to the old lab I was forced to make a slight detour. At the edge of stage 1, DeMille was making a 'miracle' for a biblical sequence in the first version of *The Ten Commandments*. Unlike his 1956 extravagance, the 1923 film was essentially a modern morality play, the tale of a corrupt contractor. The biblical scenes were included to answer, symbolically, the question posed by the central theme—is love of God greater than love of lucre? In 1923, C. B. believed that it was.

On this day Moses was receiving the authoritative Ten Commandments, and the temptation to spy on the Lord's work was too strong to resist. I pushed a flap on the huge tarpaulin tent designed to keep the sunlight out. Inside, the enclosed set was small but interesting; the tip of an ersatz, truncated mountain, some fifteen or twenty feet high, occupied no more than a few hundred feet of ground space, and on a narrow ledge near the top of the peak, Theodore Roberts, perhaps the best known and most loved character actor of his time, was perched precariously, fighting valiantly to keep his balance in the face of a man-made hurricane. While impersonating the great Jew who led his people out of that particular

Hollywood Hotel, 1903.

bondage, Roberts tightly gripped the fake marble tablets on which Yaveh's finger was to write. He was a dead image of Michelangelo's famous statue as his long white beard streamed out in the powerful blast of a wind machine, while eye searing flashes of lightning revealed him blinking in terror as he looked up toward the invisible Deity. Noisy, but fascinating—I looked for the source of the lightning.

At one side of the mountain stood a pair of "grips" manipulating a "scissors" made of twelve-foot-long two-by-fours. Carbon rods had been fastened at right angles to the scissors' upper ends, and from these insulated cables ran down to a nearby "hot-box." When the scissors were closed, then pulled apart, huge lightning-like traveling sparks were created which, in the limited space, looked like the real thing. I was impressed. However, the next day I found myself being more impressed by another man who was also recreating one of the Lord's "miracles." His name was Roy Pomeroy.

He was arguably Hollywood's master creator of "special effects" in the silent era and, rather unexpectedly for someone in his line of work, he was also the Adolphe Menjou of the back lot—a snappy dresser par excellence.

He changed clothes at least three times each day, probably four (I couldn't check on his evenings). If the Chinese are right and one picture is really worth a thousand words (an adage that modern filmmakers seem to be reversing) a portrait of Pomeroy in any of his guises would have defined the word "dapper," more precisely than did Noah Webster. His suits and shirts were impeccably tailored, his slacks and sports jackets guaranteed that summer was here, his ties were lively but smart, and his shoes were usually stylish two-tone wingtips. He must have lived nearby to make so many complete changes during his usually busy day.

Broadly speaking, there are two main branches of "special effects." One is the fabrication of fires, explosions, and other violent scenes of action on the set. The other involves the construction and manipulation of insentient forms such as dinosaurs, giant gorillas, robots, aliens (benign or malevolent), matte or glass shots, and working miniatures. Roy Pomeroy was an artist of the second kind.

Located near the old lab, Pomeroy's workshop was a magnet for a curious boy. An unprepossessing structure, it was not much larger than a modern two-car garage. Inside, on a workbench no bigger than a large refectory table, he created all of his many miracles, one of which especially impressed me in 1923.

In a rectangular, waterproofed "basin," which occupied the entire workbench, Pomeroy built a wooden, U-shaped trough about eight feet long. With the addition of an arrangement to control the flooding of the water into the basin, and a turbulent overflow into the trough, Roy brought to life the miracle of the parting and the subsequent closing of the Red Sea. This, of course, was a miniature. But the apparent size of any object on the screen is dependent on its juxtaposition to a familiar person or thing. (See Poe's, "The Sphinx.") When the shot of the miniature was superimposed over long shots of the fleeing Jews or their pursuers, the dripping walls of the parted sea appeared to tower over the tiny humans, horses, and chariots, until they finally collapsed into an angry maelstrom to properly drown the representatives of the world's most civilized society—all this, of course, to the average viewer's suspense-induced delight. (A simple film reversal of the collapsing water shot, sans Egyptians and fleeing Jews, showed the sea parting.)

By the 20th century genuine miracles were a lost art and the rod of Moses failed to protect Pomeroy. In 1928, Paramount undertook to make its first "all-talkie" and its addled executives decided that only a technical mind could cope with the complexities of the newfangled medium. Pomeroy, who, to my knowledge, had never directed drama in any form, was chosen to pilot Interference. The complexities of sound recording proved to be much simpler than the complexities of good storytelling; the film was a technical triumph but a dramatic disaster, and Pomeroy became the studio's sacrificial lamb. I never heard his name again.

In the fall of 1955 I was at Paramount filming interiors for *The Mountain*, which starred Spencer Tracy. One day we strolled out to the back lot to see a wonder the whole studio was talking about—the latest gimmick for the parting of the Red Sea in DeMille's new version of *The Ten Commandments*. I was astounded. It was a replica of Pomeroy's tabletop miniature, increased on an awe-inspiring scale.

A block-long trough of concrete had been poured; it was at least eight feet deep and thirty feet wide. Lined up along either side of the concrete ditch were a full half-dozen "water drops," huge two-story structures, with tanks at the top capable of holding thousands of gallons of water. (Such equipment was normally used in studio tanks to simulate the huge waves piled up by a hurricane at sea.) When electronically triggered, either simultaneously or in sequence, the tanks dumped their contents down steep metal slides, which curved sharply at the bottom to send the water shooting out into the trough. I had been told the concrete ditch and its waterdrops had cost three million dollars. I mentioned that to Tracy, and he shook his head in disbelief.

"God did it cheaper," he said.

Some time later I had the opportunity to see both versions of the parting of the waters. They were surprisingly similar in their total effects. However, taking his cue from God, Roy Pomeroy had done it much cheaper.

CHAPTER TWO

Only nine years after *The Squaw Man*, Hollywood was already recognized as the film capital of the United States, and it was setting its sights on the rest of the world. The first step in its remarkable progress had been a gift of nature, but it was the entrepreneurial foresight of the industry's organizers that soon placed it within reach of the "brass ring." It turned out to be pure gold.

Sunlight was fast becoming obsolete for interior lighting, but it remained essential for filming exteriors; Southern California's sun and its "great outdoors," made a winning combination. In other areas travel to distant locations was slow and costly and living conditions were primitive, but for Hollywood filmmakers such problems were easily solved. The unrivaled variety of locations, from mountain to desert to ocean, some right next door, and none more than an hour or two from the studios, made it possible to choose story material from a huge bag of genres.

The Sahara Desert, where *The Sheik* roamed, was shot on the sand dunes of a California beach, the mud and mire of *The Big Parade*, ostensibly in France, was actually filmed at "nearby" locations, and most of the classic, *All Quiet On The Western Front*, was staged and filmed on a few of Universal Studio's undeveloped acres. Nobody noticed that Robin Hood and his merry men waited to trap the rich bishop while hidden by California sycamores and live oaks. Lake Arrowhead and its surrounding mountains were the "Alps" setting for Murnau's immortal *Sunrise*, and the spectacular rock formations at Chatsworth, a half hour's ride across San Fernando Valley, was Bill Hart country. But if a greater expanse of valley and mountain were called for, the magnificent Sierra Nevada, just a morning nap in limousines for cast and crew, had the deepest canyons and the highest peaks in the continental United States. In *Old Ironsides*, the U.S.S. Constitution battled Barbary pirates in the waters off Santa Catalina Island, twenty miles across the channel from San Pedro, L.A.'s port on the Pacific.

Unquestionably, the most underrated factor leading to Hollywood's supremacy on the film beat was the superiority of "living" in Southern California. First in importance was the benign climate, with its absolute minimum of humid days or freezing nights, though a rare, out-of-state location stint was needed to appreciate Southern California's taken-for-granted near-absence of mosquitoes, chiggers, cockroaches, and other annoying insects. Finally, the environmental alternatives that were so advantageous to location hunters were also a boon to personal rest and recuperation that the stresses and strains of filmmaking made necessary. Taken together, these elements played a very large part in the establishment of an extraordinary pool of "talent-in-residence" once it had been lured here by the new opportunities to display its variety of dramatic gifts to an ever-growing audience. The salaries might have been the same elsewhere, but the fringe benefits were not.

> *Of course, earthquakes are another matter, but their injuries are primarily of the mind. Ordinarily, their rating on the charts of violence and destruction would be far below those of hurricanes, blizzards, huge river floods, and even tornados, except for one thing—while normal attacks of nature allow people to prepare their minds and their properties for the possibilities of danger and damage, the earthquake gives no warning. It is the proverbial "last thing on my mind" phenomenon, and its sudden, always unexpected revelation that even the planet under one's feet is frail and vulnerable is a trauma of the highest order. For the moment, all sense of security vanishes, leaving the ego naked indeed.*
>
> *However, I have lived in "earthquake country" for eighty years and have experienced only three quakes of significance, and only one of those has caused me any damage—a minor crack in a wall of one of my homes. Compared to the widespread destruction caused by the much more frequent floods and hurricanes, the Southern California "tremor" is a very "sometime thing."*

Quite unrelated to nature's blessings, a most important growth factor was the studio owners' unswerving attention to the business of motion pictures, which, among a multitude of concerns, meant shelling out for publicity, the exploitation of their "properties" and product, and the es-

The original Famous Players Lasky (circa 1916) lot, at Sunset and Vine. The glassed in structure—center rear—was a stage that permitted shooting in the rain.

tablishment of thousands of theaters in which to show them off. Paramount alone had perhaps nine hundred "cinemas" in the United States and Canada, and more on the way. They ranged from small "neighborhood houses" to spacious showplaces, which were being spotted in the larger cities. Enterprising developers interested only in exhibition were also building grandiose "palaces" that architects and purists dismissed as ostentatious but which seemed to charm the crowds that patronized them.

1922 was the year when Southern California, already gaining notoriety for its off-the-wall architecture, was into all things Egyptian. So it was no coincidence that in the same year Syd Grauman opened the doors of the Egyptian Theater to the public. The inaugural film was Robin Hood; *it starred Hollywood's smoothest portrayer of "derring-do," Douglas Fairbanks.*

I had surreptitiously hoarded fifty cents of my paper-route money to see my favorite actor, and that would require another deception after I got home, but I soon put that out of my mind. From Hollywood Boulevard a very wide roofless corridor, or gallery, led back some fifty or sixty yards to the lobby of the theater. On the right of the walkway was a fancy cafe-tea room called "The Pig 'n Whistle." It featured small sandwiches, chocolates, candies, and a soda fountain that dispensed the tastiest ice-cream treats in town. The shops which stood on the left of the corridor are lost to memory.

Wide-eyed, I started toward the lobby, but stopped when my attention was captured by the Bedouin on the roof. Pacing majestically along a hidden walk atop the theater, decked out in Egyptian robes and turban and carrying a long-barrelled Arabian rifle, he marched back and forth with a remarkable dignity. This sudden and unexpected sight flipped me into a subtly different world—a strange but promising "enfoldment."

The mood was only heightened when I walked into the theater. It was so clean![1] Seeming to slumber in the semi-darkness, the auditorium radiated a palpable silence. As my eyes adjusted to the dim light I looked up and around me; the rich, gilded woodwork, the ornate images on the walls, the flickering points of light on the ceiling's simulated evening sky, brought me as close to heaven as I ever expected to get. Cathedrals I have seen since are much more grand and immeasurably greater as architecture, but none has ever inspired the awe or equaled the impact of Grauman's Egyptian Theater in 1922.

With the exception of a few show places now subsidized as historic treasures, those theatrical palaces, the cathedrals, which once brought a touch of elegance and beauty into innumerable dreary lives, are gone. They have been swallowed up by myriads of small "black holes," proving that evolution is not always progress. What is not realized by the current generation of filmmakers is that with their departure a subtle yet powerful dramatic *influence has been lost, for never again will viewers respond to the stimulus of the palaces' artfully imposed "atmosphere," that near-hypnotic aura that evoked a willingness to "suspend disbelief" before a single frame of film had been seen.*

Before Hollywood could claim to be the film capital of the world, one more rung had to be climbed. And for that it needed a boost from abroad.

Hollywood was building an industry; Europe was creating an art. For those who understood the ways of the world, predicting the ultimate winner of the crown required no prescience, for even artists who scorned the marketplace soon became aware of a statistical truism: few artists are born rich. *Ergo*, most art requires sponsorship.

World War I had played havoc with royal courts and royal largesse. There were few kings, princes, or other members of the world's aristocracy remaining, and they had no resources to spare for the support of artists working in a medium whose "canvas" for a single creation cost more than earlier artists could utilize in a lifetime. Wherever possible, governments now took on the responsibilities of sponsorship, but though Germany, Russia, and France subsidized a few filmmakers, the first two countries were virtually bankrupt, and France was not much better off. Only the United States, which had lost nothing in the war except the cheapest of all materiel, manpower, was in a position to support talent, and they could do it in the traditional way, through private enterprise—and the profit system. America had the required number of viewers (including many from the world at large) who could spend the required number of dollars to assure an "in the black" operation that made possible the outright hiring, rather than the sponsoring, of artists, craftsmen, and technicians if, when, and wherever they could be found.

Animal breeders long ago learned a truth, which the aristocrats were loathe to accept; cross-breeds have certain advantages over pure-blooded stock. Hollywood's films were doing well, but aside from D. W. Griffith, Erich Von Stroheim (an Austrian), and eventually King Vidor, few American filmmakers were getting international attention. On the other side of the pond the grass looked greener; in spite of their relative poverty the Russians, the Germans, and, to a lesser extent, the French, were earning world reputations as the leading "artists" of the cinema world.

American film tycoons had always been suspicious of art, new or old, but they could never be accused of ignoring talent. They decided to emulate the cattlemen and enlarge the industry's genetic pool. It was one of the smartest moves they ever made; aside from the comics who had arrived earlier, the first "brain drain" of modern times got underway when European directors, actors, and even a few cameramen were brought to Hollywood during the "Roaring Twenties" and the early thirties.

Ernst Lubitsch arrived in 1922 at Mary Pickford's invitation. In 1925, Mauritz Stiller agreed to work in Hollywood only if his protégé, Greta Garbo, could accompany him. (In one of movie history's ironies, the "in-demand" Stiller failed, while Garbo, the unwanted, achieved an unmatched success.)

Michael Curtis shipped over in 1925, to be followed by such great directors as Murnau, Zinneman, Wilder, Wyler, Hitchcock, a number of slightly less talented filmmakers, and British actors by the score. Some of the newcomers found themselves "out of sync" with Hollywood production practices and techniques, and returned to Europe. And although for the majority who stayed California was no bed of roses, neither was it a briar patch. There were enough improbably successful immigrants to keep the "hopefuls" hoping, and immigration alive.

A number of British comedians, headed by the inimitable, though often imitated, Charlie Chaplin, were working in American studios as early as 1913, but it was not until the century's third decade that European stars and directors who had established top reputations in heavy drama began to find careers and homes in Hollywood. One of the colony's early imports was Appolonia Chalupiec, a Polish actress better known as Pola Negri. Largely under the guidance of Ernst Lubitsch, she had acquired a reputation in Berlin as an exotic and passionate femme fatale, a dramatic personality she also affected off the screen. From the day of her arrival in town she lost no time in establishing herself as the most talked-about woman in the colony. Her efforts to top all competition in flamboyance and flair did not remain unchallenged, and she was soon embroiled in a feud with Gloria Swanson, Hollywood's entrenched champion of chic.

One day, while sitting on the steps, which led into the projection booth, I interrupted my two-bit box lunch to study the arrival of a chocolate-brown Rolls Royce as it pulled into the lot. (The Rolls was not yet an everyday sight in California.) My interest turned to fascination when the smartly uniformed chauffeur opened the passenger door and Pola Negri stepped out. It must have been a cold day; she was wearing a full-length coat, a mink, whose color exactly matched that of the limousine. But what made the sight especially intriguing was that a day or two earlier, at the same spot, she had stepped out of another Rolls Royce, swathed in another fur coat, and that car was painted a pure white to match the ermine she was wearing. It was rumored that she had other cars and other matching furs, but these two "sets" were the only ones I ever saw. They were quite enough to give Negri at least a temporary advantage over Miss Swanson.

A second episode involving the Polish star was unsettling rather than fascinating, a milestone in my young life. It was the first time I heard a woman swear. Of course, every street-smart kid, in any period of history, is fully aware of what we once called "dirty words"; they are the nearly total vocabulary of adolescent humor. But a woman? In mixed company? In 1923? God forbid! That was like seeing a woman smoke in public.

Whenever there was a moment to spare I would sneak into the projection booth to learn the ropes of a promising vocation. That day, Herbert Brenon was looking at his dailies—probably for Shadows Of Paris. *(We never called them rushes then.) Negri was also in the viewing room; she was one of a few stars that could bear watching and analyzing their previous day's work. During a pause between reels my ear was glued to the booth's porthole—I had to know what the "brains" talked about. Miss Negri was vociferously voicing her opinion of some scene or performance, and the words "damn" and "Jesus Christ!" seemed to indicate negative reactions.*

Now, used as profanity, these words are hardly historic, even when uttered by a movie star. But history is more than a mere recording of characters or events frozen in time. Human character has changed little, if at all, in thousands of years—what makes Hitler different from Genghis Khan or Attila the Hun—and events have a tendency to repeat themselves. The evolution of customs and manners, however, even in such staples as war, is an essential part of history, or should be. How else to mark the difference between epochs and eras? The foregoing simple anecdote, when compared to the dialogue in almost any contemporary film or a conversation between two or more adults or sub-teenagers, can, in a matter of seconds, demonstrate the tremendous progress made in manners and attitudes in less than seventy years.

D. W. Griffith was unarguably the premier filmmaker of his time, but most of Hollywood's directors got short shrift from the critics and viewers who enjoyed their work. Shortsighted American distributors had waited too long to join Europe's push to more serious films. Even Griffith had to make his first four-reel film in secret, and wait for a year or more to see it released. Earlier, Adolph Zukor could find no exhibitors for a four-reeler featuring the "divine" Sarah Bernhardt as Queen Elizabeth; he had to organize his own distribution and production company.

Griffith's *The Birth Of A Nation* had broken the logjam. It had been deservedly praised and admired for its unprecedented technical breakthroughs, and just as deservedly criticized for its highly biased stereotypes and racial attitudes. However, it had been a financial triumph, which was what counted even then, and it jump-started America's film industry into achievements, which soon placed it at the top of the heap. By 1920, American directors were unequaled as a group, though ignored by critics who preferred the theatrically staged films of Europe. Hollywood had created a style, which made its films the envy of all who sought to profit from their work. Its filmmakers had developed, and continued to develop, a technical proficiency that soon had their European colleagues damning their work as "slick" in defense of their own largely stage-oriented output. Led by Thomas H. Ince, American producers had organized their studios beyond comparison. And their cornucopia of filmmakers and actors gave them a statistical advantage in discovering that scarcest of "needles in a haystack"—exceptional talent.

Tom Ince was one of Hollywood's most creative producers; the right man in the right place at the right time. He was a good director, an excellent producer, and a master editor. Leroy Stone, a supervising editor for whom I cut several films at Paramount in the early thirties, had served his apprenticeship at Inceville, and he had stories to tell. Ince, he said, would often put a film "on ice" for a few months. When he judged a release was timely he might rework the film by altering its temporary titles to change a wife to a sister or a mother, for instance, or by putting a different spin on the content of sequences to fit the prevailing climate. With titles, nothing was impossible. Even today, in a difficult situation, a title is not infrequently used as the last resort.

The priceless contribution of the European infusion was not in the development of filmmaking techniques, from which they got more than they gave, but in the field of culture. A study of Hollywood's creative personnel shows that most of the writers, directors, and actors of the time under consideration were born before the turn of the century.

As for their origins, a list of the outstanding filmmakers shows that they came from towns like Quincy and Carbondale, Illinois; from Cincinnati and Springfield, Ohio; St. Paul, Minnesota and Logan, Utah; from Cawker City, Parsons, and Piqua, Kansas; from Keokuk, Iowa; Corsicana, Texarkana, and Midland, Texas; from Pittsburgh and Mix Run, Pennsylvania; from Port Huron, Michigan, and Green Ridge, Missouri; from Montreal and Toronto, Canada; from Worcester, Massachusetts; and a few from Brooklyn and the Bronx in New York City.

Very few of those listed were born to wealth and its educational advantages, but all serve to illustrate America's superiority as a land of opportunity. However, given the fact that most of the country, and especially the great heartland, still suffered the effects of the Puritan Ethic, they did little to advance America's rather dubious turn-of-the-century status as a well of culture and sophistication. It is no exaggeration to say that in those areas the bourgeoisie of Paris, Vienna, Budapest, or the scattered remnants of St. Petersburg's elite would have easily outperformed the Brahmins of Boston.

The cross-breeding of European artistic philosophies and ideologies with American "visions" and techniques unquestionably led to the development of an all-embracing visual art that quickly captured the motion picture screens of the world. However, although the Europeans' home product was a positive cultural stimulus, once in Hollywood, the consequent social intercourse had a greater impact than their American product. And yet—Ernst Lubitsch, the most successful of the film immigrants, established standards of subtlety, satire, and sophistication in a series of pictures whose lessons too many modern American filmmakers still find elusive.

CHAPTER THREE

"If it's ridiculous, it isn't funny." That may not be the exact citation of Buster Keaton's dictum, but it's very close. And it says it all. It is what characterizes most Golden Age screen comedy and differentiates it from most of what has followed. Keaton was indirectly defining humor that moved people, humor which started out as a working man's diversion and wound up as a thinking man's delight, humor which produced the only figure in motion picture history universally acclaimed a "genius" in the art.

In America—especially in America—the 'teens and the twenties were distinguished by their comedies. Names associated with dramatic films were usually those of the filmmakers, Griffith, Porter, Von Stroheim, Lang. In the very early days actors were sometimes denied screen credit for fear their popularity would breed high salaries. And the actors were largely just that—actors, thespians, elocutionists. Although gesticulation was declamation's companion in the theater,[2] it was gradually played down in films, but it was not until well after the introduction of amplified sound that natural, or "honest" acting, as exemplified by Spencer Tracy, Monty Clift, and Katharine Hepburn became the standard of excellence.

Comedians, on the other hand, were being themselves; Chaplin was "Charlie" in his films, Keaton was "Buster," and so on through a formidable list. Even the era's last two great comedians called each other "Mr. Laurel" and "Mr. Hardy" more often than "Stan" and "Ollie." Consequently, the public was completely at home with the names and characters of Chaplin, Mabel Normand, Buster Keaton, Harold Lloyd, Fatty Arbuckle, Ben Turpin, Louise Fazenda, Charlie Chase, Lloyd Hamilton, and others only a little less known and loved.

Lloyd Hamilton's name is lost in the river of oblivion; in his time he was a funny man. Like most of his fellow comics he eschewed odd costumes, except for an identifying cap, and he did his own stunts, as did most of his competitors. It was a matter of pride, and Hamilton was as proud as any man who ever walked down "poverty row."

Hamilton was somewhat rotund, though not nearly as hefty as Fatty Arbuckle, but Arbuckle had the agility of a gymnast despite his extra tonnage. Hamilton was not quite that spry, and in an unlucky mishap on the set he broke one of his legs. Seventy years ago that was a serious matter. It meant weeks of hospitalization and months of convalescence.

Inevitably, the day of deliverance arrived; Hamilton limped into the Mount Sinai Hospital on Fountain Avenue and his cast was removed. He walked out with a half-forgotten spring in his stride, stopped at the top of a wide flight of steps fronting the hospital and, like a premature "Rocky" celebrating his bursting vitality, he let out a triumphant yell and tossed his redundant crutch high in the air. "What goes up must come down," and the falling crutch was too much for his not-yet-restored sense of balance. Hamilton tumbled down the steps and broke his other leg. His reaction is not a matter of record, but his misfortune was Hollywood's "thigh-slapper" for a full week. "That's our boy!" they chortled. "Anything for a laugh."

The incident says a good deal about comedy and its sources. The best is based on the most real kind of reality—a manageable situation suddenly gone awry, overweening hopes turning into headlong disasters, hubris instantly bringing about an ignominious Waterloo, "Pride goeth before a fall," the braggart forced to eat his boastful words, and sometimes the reverse, the sad-sack facing adversity with class. It is hard to imagine a sequence more deeply rooted in reality than the hunger scene in *The Gold Rush*—it's still the funniest sequence in the picture. Since that film was made more than seventy years ago, most of today's film viewers have never seen it, and the few who have will hardly recall specific scenes in detail, so a brief mention of the sequence in question will help to explain my strong admiration.

Chaplin and his sidekick, Mack Swain, have been marooned in a one-room cabin for many days by a howling, sub-arctic blizzard. They have long since run out of food, and both are desperately hungry—so hungry that Charlie boils his boots and prepares to eat them. After improvising a bib he sucks down the laces as if they were two long pieces of spaghetti, then proceeds to delicately remove the sole of one of his boots as if he were filleting a trout at Maxim's. The protruding nails closely resemble

D.W. Griffith (far right) with Mary Pickford and Charles Chaplin together for the film
Broken Blossoms, 1919.

the skeleton of a deboned fish. Meanwhile, Mack Swain, hallucinating
from hunger, sees Charlie as a man-sized chicken and, axe in hand, stalks
him around the table.

Versions of such desperate reactions to starvation have been reported
in real life in almost every generation (the Donner Party, for instance) but
Chaplin's ingeniously-crafted treatment made the scene one continuous
roll of laughter rather than a tragedy.

One theory holds that such comedy was popular because its level of
stupidity allowed the viewer to feel superior to the protagonist on the screen.
That is a cynical and superficial analysis which ignores the high level of
empathy the viewer shared with the man or woman he knew on a first name
basis; in the comedian's embarrassment he often recognized his own ineptitude artfully exaggerated, and in the artist's ultimate triumph he sometimes
saw a hoped-for life belt. At the very least, his laughter was a catharsis,
which served to put his own problems into a more acceptable perspective.

The honesty and believability of character portrayal was created by an
equivalent honesty of "performance." The viewer believed what he was

seeing on the screen when the comedian believed what he was doing on the set. This was the secret of all good comedy: no matter how unexpected or implausible the situation, the actor played it straight[3].

Raymond Griffith and the silent screen were made for each other. Whether by accident or by birth, Griffith could speak only in a hoarse whisper, a handicap that turned him into a producer when sound intruded. He had one other peculiarity: no matter what the storyline of his two-reelers, Griffith's screen character almost always wore white tie and tails. I learned from him that a man need not be tall to look elegant in a dress suit, and I learned something about film reality.

Griffith was making a film at Paramount and I sneaked onto the set to watch him in action. I came in as he and his director were discussing a plot problem: how to turn the tables on the villain who was chasing him through the house. They were in the set's bedroom, and after a moment's thought Griffith whispered, "I run in here, look around, then reach under the bed and pull out a fireman's axe."

The director shook his head. "The audience will wonder how the axe got under the bed," he said.

Griffith demurred. "If they see me pull it out," he rasped, "they'll know it was there."

And that, of course, was perfect "film" sense, which is very different from "common." I learned something else that day that all directors should heed: it pays to listen to actors. They can often make you look good.

This chapter's lead is a quotation from Buster Keaton. It is not an error. More than any comic, then or now, Keaton could articulate the comedic conceptions of his work. Chaplin, on the other hand, has been poked, probed, and plumbed for over seventy years—he also wrote more than one autobiography—yet a seeker after his "truth" will find little enlightenment about the basis of his work or the workings of his hidden mind. Virtually all available comments about the "how" of his films come from observers who try to "winkle out" his success from his final results, but not from Chaplin. That's not unusual. The wellsprings of most creation are instinct and intuition; results may be put into words but not their genesis or growth. When asked to analyze their work most artists will offer some variation of, "It seemed the only way to go." But the "way" itself is obscure, fading like a soon-forgotten dream. It is obvious that Chaplin couldn't, or didn't care to, explain, even to himself, how he arrived at his results.[4]

The Gold Rush made and released in 1925. Re-issued in 1942.

Chaplin's achievements were all the more remarkable since they were accomplished with a minimum of motion picture techniques. He seemed oblivious to developing conceptual and technological ideas and advanced little beyond the "theatrical" staging of his early years at Keystone. Not only did his lengthy "full" shots suggest the presence of a proscenium as a frame for compositions, his occasional close-ups were shot "straight on" as if viewed from a center seat in the auditorium. He always played to an imaginary viewer fixed in space, rarely taking advantage of more effective points of view.[5] (This appeared to be a lingering "style" that characterized the work of many filmmakers who learned their trade under Mack Sennett.) Chaplin's rather primitive set-ups also limited the use of cutting techniques, which were reaching unparalleled levels of effectiveness by the early 20s. His last effort as a director was *The Countess Of Hong Kong*. Made in 1966, in the afterglow of the Golden Years, it was a painful-to-watch mistake which exposed all his shortcomings and showed none of his talents.

Chaplin's genius rested on his surpassing skill in "building to a laugh," and on his creation and development of "the little tramp," perhaps the most seductive screen character of all time—a mischievous imp who was frequently cruel to his social enemies (for all of his best films were socially oriented) yet tender, loving, and forgiving to the poor, the disadvantaged, and the defeated. As a classic survivor he was admired, even loved, by the world's "little" men and women (the biggest audience available) yet his character was so universally human that even those he lampooned loved "Charlie" on the screen.

Buster Keaton was a "genius" of a different sort, a master technician who has only recently come into his own, perhaps because most of today's filmmakers feel more at home with techniques and clever gadgets than with the much more difficult field of human nature. The stony-faced comic who disdained theatrical gestures and facial distortions was as funny as Chaplin, but less empathetic; his comedy dealt more with "things" than with people; his women were stereotypical "props" with little or no influence on the plot. But if his screen character was less winsome than Chaplin's, his awareness of the technical and artistic possibilities inherent in the film medium was unsurpassed. If only those two "geniuses" could have merged their respective talents into one....

The Hollywood of the silent era's middle period owes a great deal to Chaplin, Keaton, Lloyd, Langdon, and many others, not only for their talents, which collared much of the world's market, but for their contributions to its technology and for their spawn. Their work culminated in the semi-sophisticated sound films of Capra, Stevens, McCarey, and others who learned the rudiments of their trade at Keystone. What university can claim better graduates than that?

CHAPTER FOUR

A messenger boy with few messages to deliver is on very thin ice. Famous Players was a profit-oriented company whose charitable instincts might not survive its next box office flop. In such a precarious situation the only insurance was an indispensable position, and those were not easy to find. Fortunately, before the film factories became essentially rental lots, each studio was a small walled city, which could supply all the necessities of life. The obvious film stages and equipment housing aside, it had its own hospital, doctor, and nurses, as well as a restaurant, garages with a complete staff of expert mechanics to service all its limos and supply trucks, and clothes-makers of all sorts, including designers who for many years set the fashions for the entire world.

Yes, one could be born, live, and even die without straying too far from the studio, for the nearest cemetery for the accommodation of those who had completed life's apprenticeship was just over the north wall which separated Paramount and RKO from the rest of Hollywood. And although all these advantages were not yet available in 1923, each studio still teemed with every imaginable sort of laborer, artisan, artist, and professional; an ambitious person already within its walls could always turn up something. Not being finicky about the status of that "something" made the search a good deal easier.

Across the street a true laboratory with state-of-the-art equipment and ultra-modern conveniences was still months away from completion. Our old lot was in the final stages of obsolescence. The single projection room was small and stuffy, the booth equipment antiquated. The "sample copy room," which also housed the film cutters, was a relic of the nickelodeon era, and in this fossilized environment I found a short-term and a long-term opportunity.

The cutters, as film editors were then called,[6] occupied a balcony, four or five feet wide, which jutted out of a wall of the sample copy room at a height of eight or nine feet. Six or seven cutters sat elbow to elbow at their silent movieolas, separated from each other only by their "trim bins."[7] Splicing equipment was not yet available, at least not in our snuggery, and the cutters fastened their chosen "cuts" end-to-end with paper clips while winding them up on a reel, then passed the loaded reels on to the girls below the balcony to be spliced and readied for viewing. I convinced the cutters, who were all women at Famous Players, that they could drop the reels to me and save themselves the trouble of a trip down the stairway, which was some distance from their workplace.

Fifty yards south of Selma Avenue a short, dead-end alley connected Argyle Avenue with Stage 1. It functioned as a sidewalk for studio workers and as a driveway for the occasional delivery trucks. It was walled in on the south side by Pomeroy's workshop and the camera loading and repository rooms, and on the north by our bob-tailed lab, the projection viewing room, a small cubicle where hand coloring was laboriously done, and a couple of scruffy offices. Where the alley mouth kissed Argyle Avenue a young black boy, perhaps a year or two my senior (how can one tell whether the appearance of age comes from the years lived or the conditions of life?) sold afternoon newspapers. It was a good corner. He had a reliable and, in the tradition of show business, a liberal clientele; directors, actors, and crew members entering and exiting the projection room, and workers leaving for home at the day's end. He was a thin, cynical, and somewhat bitter kid, much wiser than I, and an excellent sketch artist. I had lived in a largely black area just off Central Avenue, I had played with black kids at racially-mixed schools without any awareness of ethnic prejudice—color was simply part of nature's kaleidoscope. Yet I took it for granted he would never have the opportunity to give his gifts full rein. We talked often, and we played catch in the alley with the ball and gloves he always brought with him. And that's how the cutters knew they could trust me to catch their loaded reels, which was step one in my planned campaign for indispensability.

Fat books have been written about the thousands of "things," technically laborsaving but often more stress inflicting than beneficial, that have blessed our civilization throughout the 20th century. As noted, seventy years

Dmytryk editing Mae West's *Belle of the Nineties* (1934). Roy Stone was the
editorial supervisor. I always cut on the silent moviola (on the metal plate
to my right in the picture).

ago film at Famous Players was still spliced by hand—and mouth. The
operation involved the ubiquitous single-edged safety razor blade, a little
saliva spread by the tongue to soften the emulsion to be scraped off the film,
and a dab of cement to carefully glue the scene ends together. A year later
we were using splicing machines, which eliminated razor blades but mandated the use of carbon-tetrachloride for cleaning the machines' slicing blocks.
Many decades later came tape splicing—neater, faster, more convenient—
and colorless.[8] For those few left who have come up through the ranks, the
taste of emulsion, the odor of banana oil, carbon-tet, and film cement are
the nostalgic equivalents of the legitimate theater's "smell of greasepaint."
Losing them is like excising a vibrant color from the rainbow. That in itself
is certainly no loss to those who have never "smelled the flowers," but it
symbolizes a more damaging deprivation: increased simplification and ro-
botization have practically eliminated those compulsory exercises in ingenuity and resourcefulness, which served to sharpen artistic creativity. And
that has been a noticeable loss indeed.

Catching reels and splicing film was short-term insurance; the new laboratory's plans called for up-to-date cutting rooms, which would make the tossing of reels follow the dodo bird. Something with a longer life span was needed. As often happens, the recognition of a need brought its solution—the realization that habit was one of the most tenacious traits of the human character came with my awareness of the addicts who required a smoking siesta every half hour or so. There was as yet no public opposition to smoking, but film was built on a nitro-cellulose base that was extremely flammable. It had already been the cause of several catastrophic fires, and smoking was strictly prohibited in any room that contained film. At peak working hours those who smoked had to rely on relief workers when the inevitable urge demanded assuagement. That had worked to my advantage in the sample copy room. Now it greatly extended the area of opportunity.

The projection machine (or projector, for short) is what brings the static frames of the film's image to life, and the projection mystique had intrigued me from the day I had first stuck my head into the projection booth. A studio projectionist's work schedule was normally spasmodic, but not infrequently he was required to run dailies, cut reels, or features, for a non-stop two hours or more. At those times he was not free to leave the projector, since a badly-made splice or a worn work print might break; fire was an ever-present possibility.

Our projectionist, a gaunt, funereal man named Mr. Glasscock, was a very heavy smoker, with no one to back him up. Noticing my avid interest, he was quick to realize that salvation was at hand. He assured me I was always welcome and wasted no time in teaching me the ropes, which, in the total absence of automation, were not easy to learn.

The projector was an old Powers, with a carbon arc lamp-house. The source of light was a crater in one of the two carbon rods, and keeping it centered and burning evenly demanded the nearly constant manipulation of seven knobbed controls which, between them, moved either the upper or the lower carbon rod, or both, in any or all of the three dimensions. Sometimes it was more than two hands could easily manage. However, within a couple of weeks Mr. Glasscock could take a few minutes off whatever the emergency. Then the struggle started.

Who knew when a cutter would have to drop a reel, and Mr. Baldridge wanted me always on the ready in the sample copy room. There was no record of the number of times I was yanked out of the projection booth and ordered never to enter it again, or the corresponding number of times I risked my job by disobeying his orders. But Glasscock refused to give up cigarettes, and in the busy hours of late afternoon he needed relief. When the summer vacation rolled around and I was working full time for sixteen dollars a week, the boss graciously admitted defeat. I was nearly fifteen, and a studio projectionist; thank heaven there was no studio or labor law to say me nay. For in that decrepit projection booth I learned one of the most important lessons of my professional life. It came from the projector—a move into the "fourth dimension"—a dramatic artifice specific to motion pictures that helped to make Hollywood filmmakers preeminently popular, an artifice that only Hollywood filmmakers seem to understand, though the concept can be expressed in one word—*pace*.

It started with American comedies and westerns. High speed action, extending to a frequent use of "undercranking" in chases,[9] was the one thing they had in common. Perhaps because so many of Hollywood's early directors went the comedy route, which had been developed to the nth degree by Mack Sennett and his team, pace was a key ingredient of most Hollywood films until that generation had passed on or retired. A single example will make the point.

Frank Capra spent most of his twenties with Hal Roach, Mack Sennett, and Harry Langdon as a gag man, writer, and director. His work is still admired by the young as well as the old. Compared to the few modern films of substance, his pace could be described as "furious." Never do his actors indulge in long "method" reactions as if the lines they hear are from Emmanuel Kant or Carl Jung. Capra knew that few lines in any film are profound, nor are they intended to be—the message is more in the characters' behavior than in their words. And it cannot be denied that his pictures carried messages and morals. These were not dished up as modern revelations, a la "Proverbs," but bit by bit throughout the length of the picture. They were delivered almost subliminally within the "cover" of enjoyable material, which, like a jigsaw puzzle, became clear with its final assembly. That was the essence (and apparently now the lost secret) of successful filmmaking—"Make 'em laugh, make 'em cry, but always keep 'em entertained." Today few people read Kant, a fact that troubles only those who do, but millions avidly view *It's A Wonderful Life*. Fifty years old, ancient for a film—and not exactly faultless, it is still going strong—and fast. Even Jimmy Stewart's engaging stammer enhances the pace.

While Capra, McCarey, Stevens, LaCava, and others were learning the value of pace through comedy, I was taking lessons from a machine. Silent projectors had a speed control. It was the projectionists' standing joke that if they needed a few bucks in overtime they could cut down the running speed; if they wanted to get home early, they would run the film at a faster pace than normal. The operative word here is "normal." Most film historians know little of projection booths or their mechanical equipment. They do, however, know that the normal silent camera speed was sixty feet per minute.[10] They assume that the same must have been true of projection speed. Not so—at least not during my apprenticeship.

Normal speed for projecting silent films was seventy-two feet per minute, one-fifth faster than the speed at which they had been shot. That was not the result of some projectionist's whim. It was arrived at empirically by the directors who noticed their efforts played better at that speed. In keeping with nearly everything else in the art of filmmaking, reality did not "play" real. Puzzling over that paradox I eventually hypothesized that within the confines of an auditorium that eliminates the many intrusions of the outside world, the viewer's attention was so monopolized by the life on the screen that movement, reaction, and, later, dialogue were more quickly grasped and assimilated. Whether the reasoning is sound or not, the results speak for themselves. Many a film student has wondered at the vitality of the old classics; it was certainly *not* the result of technical excellence, which was not up to today's standards. But when the necessities of sound eliminated speed control and naturalized acting pace, the early filmmakers made up the difference by developing a skill at coaxing livelier performances out of actors, without obvious rushing. It is still true, though rarely realized except in action pictures, that an increase of ten to fifteen percent in a scene's pace will look natural, yet play with increased vitality.[11] Which is one of the developments that made our "shadow medium" the world's most dynamic and popular art form.

CHAPTER FIVE

It can be sympathetically depicted, realistically presented, or crudely inflicted; it can be eulogized, satirized, or trivialized, but the essence of any film, good, bad, or indifferent, is life and the world that supports it. Although much of a person's knowledge of life and the world is acquired through viewing, reading, and instruction, experience is the seasoning that brings truth and substance to the stew. To experience the world you must see it through your own eyes and, unless you are a born hobo, it can be costly. Experiencing life (which is unavoidable) is much more important. It can also be much cheaper; just find a prime vantage point and watch life go by. Hollywood has often been accused of excessive nepotism, but most of its successful artists have traveled the low road. Fortunately, seventy years ago apprenticeship was still a general practice, and for an apprentice a studio projection booth was an ideal perch for the study of the human species.

It was an uncrowded field. Although many projectionists find it a satisfying occupation, few get into it by choice. In the studios, however, opportunity lurked behind every projection-booth door and at every projection-booth porthole. There was the opportunity to meet directors, producers, music composers and, a few years later, sound engineers and electronic experts. There was also the opportunity to come into contact with actors, not only as artists but as people. (I met Mary Brian at the projection-booth door when she came in to see a day's rushes of *Peter Pan*, in which she was playing Wendy. We were both fifteen, and we became lifelong friends.) Most important, there was the inescapable opportunity to work, in a sense, with the studio's film editors; it was through them that a projectionist could view and review the work of all the others. He ran, and watched, if he wished to do so, the original dailies, which more-or-less indiscriminately displayed the talents of the directors, the

37

photographers, the actors, and the set designers; he watched as scene and "take" selections were made. Later he could see portions of those discrete selections being combined into a coherent whole, and follow them as they were realigned and reedited into a dramatic continuity. He could also observe the editorial choices of the directors and/or producers as they reworked the editors' cuts. And throughout this ever-recurring process he was able, if he were so inclined, to make his own step-by-step judgments and test them against those made by the artists who carried the responsibility for their decisions. The final opportunity allowed him to evaluate his assessments, to learn a good deal about dramatic structure, to differentiate between "acting" a character and "being" one, to recognize the difference between staging for the theater and staging for the screen, and to develop his tastes. All these opportunities were there, not knocking, just waiting to be recognized. But very few projectionists cared to "seize the moment."

Insecurity was rarely a problem for the projectionists I knew. They were totally unambitious; an odd lot, but very interesting. Most were clones of the man who has found a job that is not too taxing, carries few responsibilities, and offers moderate hours and good pay—all of which can add up to a lifetime of contentment. They were unaspiring, but not unintelligent, and they usually had interesting hobbies. Among those I knew, one was a skilled and original woodcarver; one renovated antique automobiles; one was a writer who never published, nor did he care to; one was, in a sense, a scholar—his eclectic curiosity made him an omnivorous reader in many fields, and he could probably have published, but that would have made him accountable, which was a contradiction of his philosophy of life. Oh, yes, one led perhaps the definitive carefree existence—he spent every spare moment on the beach, as brown as a dark roast coffee bean.

Many of those whom the projectionists served found them enigmatic, which some consider the equivalent of profound. I became aware of an item of Hollywood folklore in the making when a director asked me what I thought of a sequence I had just run for him. I was young enough to be embarrassed by such a question, but not quite old enough to be politic, and I asked him why he wanted my opinion. He laughed. "Up front," he said, "many think that projectionists develop an instinct for what makes a film popular."

I felt that implied a mediocre taste. "If that's true," I countered, "why don't they let one of us run the studio?"

He laughed a little louder. I still had to learn what depths of insecurity are present in every creator.

It could have been in the fall of 1923, the spring of 1924, or some time between the year's most pleasant seasons when the new lab, an honest-to-goodness film laboratory, welcomed its occupants to the rooms and cubbyholes where many would spend the rest of their working lives. Compared to the old lab it was a monster, four stories high and covering only a little less than a quarter of a city block. The first two floors were reserved for a studio lab's proper functions: developing both negative and positive film, using the prints of one to create the other, making reprints and release prints, and storing negative which had been exposed in the shooting.

The old lab personnel was transported to the third floor nearly lock, stock, and barrel—somehow Baldridge had been lost in the shuffle, and so was Glasscock, but in those days of rapid studio expansion a good projectionist, like a good short-order cook, could find work almost anywhere at any time. I always assumed, or hoped, that my mentor had found himself one step closer to the job every projectionist dreams about.

Much of the third floor was occupied by a new and much larger sample copy room, and by a long string of completely equipped cutting rooms, each of which accommodated a single cutter who would no longer have a curious associate looking over her shoulder when she worked.

"Looking over a shoulder"—that can be a most intimidating situation. Take Henry Hathaway, for instance. Ordinarily he was a pleasant gentleman, but he was renowned for his tightly-strung nerves and his hair-trigger temper when on the set. He was on location in Wall Street and, as he should have expected, office workers were hanging out of high office windows by the hundreds, watching him filming a scene. Henry's blood approached the boiling point and the crew waited for him to blow his top. Suddenly he leaped from his chair, glared up at the skyscrapers, and screamed, "I don't look over your shoulders when *you* work!" He was in New York, and it is doubtful that he really got anyone's attention.

At the center of the third floor was the heart of it all—the delivery area where the labor of hundreds of men and women finally came to life on the screen. Four projection rooms, each nearly as large as a unit of a modern multiple group theater, shared two long projection booths. Each booth had two projection-machine complexes to service its two auditoriums. The lamp-houses contained Mazda lamps and once the switch lever was pulled they required no skill to operate. That left a lot of time for reading, playing chess, studying, or dawdling. I was still the "relief man," but now we had two full-time operators and a chief projectionist who took care of the bookings and supervised his miniscule kingdom.

Production on the Vine Street lot continued through the mid-'20s. At the same time some of it was being shunted at an increasing tempo to a new and much larger studio on Marathon Avenue, just south of Hollywood Cemetery. Offices, enclosed stages, and work areas were being modernized or built from scratch, and with the advent of sound all production was centralized at what, starting in 1927, was called Paramount Famous Lasky Corporation. (By 1930, The Jesse L. Lasky name disappeared from Paramount.) But until 1928 most of its cutters still worked at the lab, and the dailies, the cut sequences, and the finished prints were being viewed there. Then the silents, incapable of even a whimper, sadly but decently died, and so did the Vine Street lot. However, some of the triumphs, the crimes, and the practices witnessed during the last pentad of its existence are worthy of being recorded for posterity.

Triumph and crime are sometimes intertwined, and this condition was suffered by many of the great films out of Europe. One of the privileges and occasional pleasures of a studio projectionist was the opportunity to sit at his porthole and watch European productions soon after they were completed—to see them as they were meant to be seen. Such an opportunity usually came months, often years before they were released in the United States.[12] It was during this interval that a crime often occurred. Two films that deserve special mention will serve as examples of many others.

The first triumph, directed by E. A. DuPont, was Variety, *made in Germany in 1925. It was a powerful story of retributive justice until an anonymous American criminal, masked as a distributor, chose to edit it to his own taste. Briefly, in flashback, the original version related the story of an aerialist, the "catcher" in a high-wire act that played the small circuses. The character was realized, somewhat theatrically, by Emil Jannings. Early in the film he and his wife charitably take in a homeless but attractive derelict, played by Lya DePutti. Inevitably, Jannings falls in love with the girl and deserts his wife and family. As a team, these two achieve great success, then DePutti becomes infatuated with a younger and more handsome performer. In a jealous rage, Jannings lets DePutti slip from his fingers to her death, and winds up in jail.*

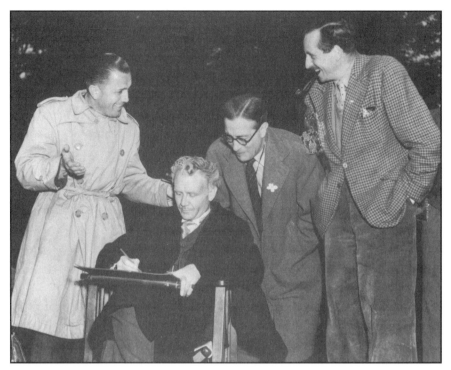

A rare photo indeed! Four Masters of Their Art. Left to right: Edward Dmytryk – film director. John Mills – actor. Freddie Young – cameraman. Bill Williams – art director. Working in England, 1946.

Some American distributor edited out the first act, beginning the film after Jennings and DePutti are already married—nothing is seen or known of a previous wife and family. The picture becomes a tale of sexual delinquency and jealousy that was already a film cliché in 1925. Whereas the original carried a story of near-biblical retribution, a story that any ancient Greek brought forward in time would have recognized as a classic tragedy, the distributor chose to make it a trite tale of deceit.

(Many years later Variety's *director, E. A. DuPont, dropped into my office. This gifted man was now a small-time agent trying to place some small-time actors. I found it difficult to speak to him without a show of emotion.)*

Sunrise, *directed by that great filmmaker Friedrich Murnau, was made in Hollywood, but it was also diminished by the distributors or exhibitors sometime during its run. At one point in the film, George O'Brien, playing a young peasant enamored of a sophisticated playgirl vacationing in the mountains, plans to drown his peasant wife, played by Janet Gaynor, as they cross a lake on their way to a day in the city. In his awkward attempt at uxoricide he succeeds only in scaring her half to death. Recovering from his moment of madness, he pleads for forgiveness, but Gaynor refuses to so much as look at him. As the boat nears the shore she leaps out and runs to the streetcar that will take them down the mountain. O'Brien follows her as she makes her way through the length of the car until she reaches the front window. Through it the distant town grows larger as the trolley makes its way down the mountain, while in the foreground O'Brien and Gaynor stand as close to the motorman as she can get. Unable to speak in the presence of this stranger, O'Brien pleads silently while she avoids his every effort at contact and communication. The scene continues in a single set-up until they jump off the streetcar at the first stop in town. It is one of the finest examples of purely cinematic art extant, or so I thought until I saw the film in a theater some years later. A scene that should have been seen and studied by every student of films had been excised, sacrificed to someone's love for mediocrity.*[13]

Between 1915 and 1928 most young people got their first taste of classical music while watching silent movies. Almost every film had a chase, clamorously sustained by the Overture from *William Tell.* "The March of the Toreadors" was reserved for martial themes, while less highbrow tunes served the sentimental sequences; "Hearts and Flowers" brought out the handkerchiefs, while "The Dream" evoked romance. In the larger theaters scores were played on the Wurlitzers, but even the scruffiest movie house in the smallest town found the local church pianist moonlighting for pin money and giving rein to her musical frustrations while banging away on an indifferently tuned upright. The important palaces, however, could afford orchestras, especially for hard-ticket showings, and orchestras required a score to accompany each film.

In the last few years of the silent era, three films were scored at the Famous Players lab: *The Wanderer*, directed by Raoul Walsh; *Old Ironsides*, directed by James Cruze; and *Abie's Irish Rose*, made by Victor Fleming, who, some ten years later, directed *Gone With The Wind*. (Nothing so startlingly illustrates the artistic and technical improvement of Hollywood films and filmmakers as a comparison of these two pictures.) The scoring procedure was quite different from those currently in use.

Only three men were involved: a composer, a word used loosely, since his function was to select and edit portions of other men's compositions; and a pianist, who played the various selections and served as a bouncing board for the composer. These two worked through the night, not timing their sequences as is now customary, but working to the film, which required the services of a projectionist for eight or ten weeks. I had no family and no social life to speak of so I became the logical choice for the third working member of the group.

The first step was to view the film as a whole, usually more than once. That was followed by a lengthy conference. Then the serious work began: the creation of a score, which started with the film company's logo and stopped only with the fade-out of the end title. The sessions usually lasted from 6:30 or 7:00 p.m. until 5:00 in the morning.

During the scoring of two of these features I was a student at the California Institute of Technology and lived in Pasadena at the Kappa Gamma (Gnome Club) fraternity house. That was ten or twelve years after Frank Capra, a fraternity brother, had been graduated from Cal-Tech as a chemical engineer. (No, there were no film classes at the Institute.) There were also no freeways yet in Southern California, and the pre-dawn drive from Hollywood to Pasadena in my beat-up Model T roadster, over an extremely tortuous two-lane highway, was a life-endangering challenge.

On more than one occasion I awoke as I pulled up at the fraternity house with absolutely no recollection of negotiating the steep-sided curves past Eagle Rock. My hair would stand on end and I would promise myself never to do it again, and after my late classes, which often lasted until 5:00 in the afternoon, I would make my way back to Hollywood and try to stay alert during the long, long night. When the musicians stopped for their midnight supper, I napped. That may have been a major turning point in my life. It was probably then I decided it was safer to stay in one place, and that Hollywood and films were more exciting than Pasadena and mathematics.

Every foot of silent film was supported by music consisting of bits and pieces selected from symphonies, operas, folk music, and any other musical form found in the public domain. These were first discussed by the two musicians, then tested for length against the scene or sequence they were underscoring, and occasionally rejected while other selections were tried. In the end a section would be set and, following the writing of a "bridge," the following section would be attacked. And so it proceeded, bit by bit and week by week, long after none of us wanted to ever see the film again.

However, more routine watching of a film can be educational in a way that has nothing to do with film technique, especially if the film consists of rushes, which differ from day to day. Trying to judge a filmmaker's character by studying his work as it unfolded on the screen was a harmless game worth playing. "Wild Bill" Wellman, for instance, was a fiery, ebullient man, as his nickname implied. He made a number of excellent films, but there are times when a "hot script" will inexplicably turn to ashes. When that happened, Wellman wilted; as his own fire cooled his boredom became evident on the screen. By the end of the third week even a non-prophetic projectionist could sense his surrender. On the other hand, the apparently impassive Austrian, Erich von Stroheim, was a different story, but his work, too, mirrored his personality. He could, and did, apply himself with unflagging interest and with no noticeable diminution in his quiet enthusiasm.

In 1926 or 1927, von Stroheim invaded the Paramount Famous Lasky lot to make *The Wedding March*. His dailies were a joy to watch; rich in detail, exciting in content, and beautifully photographed by Hal Mohr and Ben Reynolds.

Reynolds was a narcoleptic and some eight or ten years later he was shooting a B western for Paramount. Henry Hathaway was the director and I was the editor. Ben was a top lighting man, but as soon as he completed his chores and sat down to rest he would drop into a deep and noisy sleep. His misfortune was that he suffered from a troublesome disease; his good fortune was his acknowledged artistry. He was too good to be "put away," and the studio hired an extra assistant cameraman whose only duty was to keep Ben awake while the scene was being shot. It is pleasant to remember that once upon a time, even on a B western, money was not the most important element in the making of a film.

Von Stroheim's dailies continued to delight us day after day, week after week, and month after month. But even a von Stroheim had to reach the end of a schedule, and that was a movie in itself.

It came to me at second hand from George Nichols, Jr., one of Hollywood's great editors, with whom I worked for a few months as an assistant. George Nichols, Sr. was a well-known character actor. In The Wedding March *he played a wealthy soap tycoon, the father of Zasu Pitts, whom the impoverished aristocrat, played by von Stroheim, was to marry.*

Conveniently last on von Stroheim's schedule was a stag party scene. Hundreds of extras dressed as aristocrats, dashing army officers, assorted Viennese gentlemen, and women of many nations in dazzling costumes, filled the stage. When the camera stopped turning von Stroheim restocked the set with food and champagne, locked the stage doors, and hosted a "wrap party" to end all wrap parties. The shooting was finished but the party's schedule was open-ended.

Until fate took a hand.

George Nichols, Sr. was an alcoholic with a weak heart. On the third day of the orgy he, died. The party died with him. Nichols, Jr. swore to avenge his father if given the opportunity, but I felt his hatred was a touch-off target. It was liquor, food, and "fun" that killed his father, not von Stroheim.

Von Stroheim took refuge in his cutting room for a number of weeks. He emerged with a true embarrassment of riches, which, for him, was no contradiction. His first cut was carted, not carried, into the projection booth. 126 reels long, it occupied two full days of running time. Rarely tedious, often exciting, it was always interesting. One sequence alone, in which von Stroheim, dressed as an officer of Franz Josef's guard, sits his horse during an imperial parade and flirts with a village girl, played by Fay Wray, who stands nearby, ran for two reels! That was a half-hour of silent footage, and completely unreasonable even at that stage of the editing. But it was a brilliant lesson in montage that I have never forgotten.

Although there were other remarkable sequences in the first cut, this was a classic case of too much of a good thing, not enough objectivity and, more than anything else, it was a striking example of an artist enthralled by his own work. This affliction is not uncommon in a filmmaker's world, but never since Pygmalion and Galatea was it so extreme. Von Stroheim worked on the film for about six more months and succeeded in cutting it down to 60 reels, or about ten hours of running time. Politely, the studio removed him and turned the material over to Paul Weatherwax, who shaved it down to 26 reels. Eventually, it was split into two films. The first, *The Wedding March*, was a complete failure; the second, titled *The Honeymoon*, was never seen in the United States.

Sic transit gloria mundi.

Some time after the fiasco von Stroheim visited the cutting rooms and stopped at the projection booth door to talk with me. During our brief conversation he looked directly into my eyes and listened as politely as he spoke. In a matter of minutes he made a boy feel like an intelligent and fully-grown human being. Who could forget such a man and such a moment?

CHAPTER SIX

"It won't work! It's an interesting idea, but it will never work. The sound is scratchy—hardly understandable—and the…"

Dr. Robert Millikan was positively negative. It was the autumn of 1926, and we were a small group of freshmen enjoying a get-acquainted tea with the president of Cal-Tech, who was describing a recent Warner Brothers demonstration of film that "talked." Just three years after winning the Nobel Prize for weighing the electron (which was quite a trick since it couldn't be seen with the most powerful microscopes) he was not only pessimistic about the future of sound pictures, he was sure his pessimism was justified. (Remembering the incident some years later reminded me of the 19th-century scientist who proved beyond any doubt that a bumblebee couldn't fly.) But within three years that impossible sound, though still scratchy and loaded with electronic noise, was not only serviceable but often more understandable than the pristine tracks of today.[14]

One of the miracles of sound was not so much the sound itself; after all, talking pictures date back to the days of Thomas Edison, and there had been a number of attempts to synchronize sound (on records) with picture. Even short newsreels had been shown in the few theaters that had installed the requisite sound equipment. Considering these efforts the reluctance of the industry to undertake a collaborative development of the emerging methodology may be hard to understand, but in the end it was jolted out of its lassitude by a dose of free enterprise.

However, if you couldn't grab a Millikan how were you going to catch the world's interest? Warners supplied the answer when some genius realized that the product needed a "…spark, (a) flame that would kindle the public's imagination and enthusiasm."[15]   That spark was applied by the tremendous vitality and magnetic personality of an entertainer—Al Jolson.

Warners' competitors may not have understood the electron but they understood Al Jolson and show business; with the notable exception of Charles Chaplin, most of Hollywood's wheels realized that a ravenous appetite had been aroused. The problem was to satisfy it. For a while panic reigned on several fronts; while the companies and independent theater owners fought to equip their houses for sound, the few manufacturers of recording systems and sound projectors, with no inventories to fall back on, worked overtime to fill an inundation of orders.

Once sparked into awareness, however, the rapidity with which the large, established industry and its executives, artists, and craftsmen implemented the development of the radically new skills and techniques while skipping hardly a beat, was a minor miracle indeed. Paramount's Marathon lot rose to the occasion, furnishing two major theaters and four smaller rooms for the immediate needs of dailies and editing. The editors, the sample copy room personnel, and the projectionists were transferred from the lab to a permanent two-story camera and editing building, where they set about learning the functions and the operations of the revolutionary equipment.

The impressive new projection machines had sprouted an appendage, a turntable for Warners' Vitaphone records; the film projection heads were fitted with light slits and photoelectric cells for Movietone prints;[16] while Westrex sound, recorded on its own separate strip of 35mm film, was run on 'dummies' which, quite logically, delivered dialogue and music but no picture. Their motors were synchronized by induction from the master motors that ran the film projectors. This new machinery gave rise to a host of unpredictable problems, few of which could be solved on the basis of previous experience.

In keeping with "Finagle's Law," the Vitaphone record needles often skipped a groove. After a moment of utter consternation the projectionist had to figure out whether it had skipped backward or forward, which could only be done by looking through the porthole at the moving image on the distant screen. His decision was never easy, nor always right, but having made it he would "slip" the record forward on the turntable or hold it back with a slight pressure until something resembling a rubbery sync was attained. Both operations demanded some finesse, but there was no other recourse until the reel ran out.[17]

As for the dummy operation, induction motors occasionally ran amok—so did the projectionist! Acting as an independent dynamo, the motor would suddenly accelerate with frightening speed and a screaming whine, threatening to fly apart from its centrifugal momentum.

The Movietone films were relatively trouble-free, though not in the cutting room, but there was now a seven-foot high wall panel loaded with vacuum tubes that required the services of an electronic technician. Although the march of progress had simplified one item—the projector's new arc lamp houses were completely automatic—the system's ramifications easily won the day. We were all rank amateurs running highly professional equipment, and no, it was not always a "charge," for there were also many non-technical hang-ups.

Unlike the industries spawned by sound, the studios did have inventories. It had always been their custom to stay ahead of the market's needs, but their backlog now consisted only of silent films threatened with obsolescence, while a rapidly growing number of houses were ready for sound. Once more necessity was brought to bed; she birthed an ingenious idea that saved the day by solving both problems.

The truly silent films, in meaningful numbers, were made in Russia. With a viewer population that was 909 illiterate, titles were more an intrusion than a help, and they were usually omitted.[18] In the United States the silents almost always "talked"—at least the actors did. The average silent film probably counted more footage in photographed titles than in photographed images, which gave birth to a short-lived pair of experts—the "writer-editor team." It was exactly what the words suggest, a twosome composed of a writer who specialized in the genre at hand, and an editor who recomposed the film to fit their joint visions. Between them they could often improve a crude original storyline and whip the rough-cut into an enjoyable feature. Norman McCleod, a gag-man and writer, whose "stick" cartoons frequently enhanced his comedy titles, often worked in tandem with George Nichols, Jr., one of Hollywood's most creative editors. When the field dried up, McCleod turned his skills to directing comedies, Topper *and several Crosby-Hope Road pictures among them. A few years later Nichols followed in McCleod's footsteps.*

What seemed for a brief moment a catastrophe for title writers became a new bonanza. The studios found their cupboards bare of scripts for sound; a few ideas jotted down on a Brown Derby tablecloth, which players could act out while mouthing anything that came to mind, would no longer suffice. The words they now spoke had to have some continuity and make some sense. Even proven plays, which was the first material filmmakers reached for, had to be adapted to the screen, and often the title writer, experienced in movie structure, was the best person for the job. But such work was for the future, and in the meantime the theaters were getting ahead with their sound installations, and the viewing public could not be kept in a state of hopeful anticipation for an indefinite length of time. The studios' brilliant solution, which seemed quite simple once the switch was flicked, was the construction of a series of hybrid films—created by the injection of a few dialogue scenes into the silent pictures still awaiting release.

I worked as a set projectionist on several such productions; all followed the same routine. Specific scenes, essentially all dialogue, were chosen for reshooting; their sets were rebuilt, the original players recalled, along with the camera crew. The silent version of the scene to be recreated would be thrown on a small screen by a portable projector. The director who had to match the action, the photographer and his gaffer who had to match the lighting, and the actors who had to match the mood would watch as the scene was rerun as often as necessary.

The longer shots were usually salvaged from the silent film, and the director had to decide which scenes could carry dialogue. Sometimes only a few close shots were needed; sometimes the entire scene would be played from scratch in a number of set-ups. But one thing was always the same; the pressure to get the hybrids into the theaters was so great that "overtime" was a meaningless word. For *The Canary Murder Case*, which featured Louise Brooks, the dialogue pickups were directed by Frank Tuttle, who had had theatrical experience at Yale. At one session we all worked three days and two nights without going home. At thirty-seven cents an hour, straight time, I felt I was getting rich, but that was the only positive in the entire experience. And few people outside the stages were aware of the problems faced and overcome by men and women who gave far beyond the call of duty.

For starters, there was not a sound stage in town!

Convenience had dictated that the studios be built near main streets that were getting busier and noisier as L.A.'s acromegalic growth proceeded unchecked, but the noise had not bothered the silents. However, the primitive microphones of primitive sound were more sympathetic to background noise than to dialogue, so a primitive solution was attempted. The thin walls of every silent stage were draped from ceiling to floor with

1946 in England. Director Edward Dmytryk (left) and John Mills study a bit of sketched action before filming a scene of *So Well Remembered*, RKO-Rank production in which Mills heads an Anglo-American cast which also stars Martha Scott, Patricia Roc, Trevor Howard and Richard Carlson.

thick blanket-like material, which did little to deaden the sounds of the street but a lot to promote suffocating heat and dead air. They only accelerated the "wilting factor" of crews and casts.

Aircraft were an especially troublesome source of unmuffled sound, and in an effort to divert errant fliers, large bright orange balloons were tethered above every studio. Quite naturally, they served as homing beacons to the private pilots who were beginning to fill the sky—and the next step followed logically. Since all aircraft and most heavy trucks traveled during daylight hours, nighttime shooting became the general practice, and the on-the-house midnight supper was the busiest meal of the day. And although workers still found it hard to breathe in the shrouded stages, the air they breathed was cooler, and the sound engineers, or "mixers," were happy with the improved quality of their work.

They were, perhaps, the only ones. Because the problems of sound were all-important in the competition for newer and larger audiences, the mixer was the "king of the hill." Trouble often arose when the sound man, new to the film world and unaccustomed to the filmmakers' long-established tradition of cooperation and collaboration, refused to compromise or negotiate situations, which encroached on other workers' areas. Even the director occasionally gave way if his staging did not accommodate optimum mike placement.

The development of the overhead mike-boom made the mixer's and the director's work somewhat easier, but it was only another thorn in the photographer's side. He could light around a mike concealed in a vase of flowers or a telephone, but the boom's long, floating arm, with its huge, pendulous microphone, cast shadows in all directions. Relighting for this condition was difficult and time-consuming, and rarely an acceptable solution; an inferior lighting configuration always resulted in an inferior picture. There were bruised egos and hot arguments in plenty, which the sound mixer usually won.

The photographer's suffering was aesthetic, but his operator's distress was physical. The three-camera system, which became the norm, was devised to minimize the time required to light three different set-ups by shooting them as one. But it is impossible to obtain maximum photographic quality when using one lighting plan for three different angles, and once more quality was sacrificed to quantity. Of course, some sacrifices had to be made, and under normal circumstances that might have been just one more nagging, though minor, problem, but cameras were noisy and individual blimps had not yet been developed.[19] The short-term solution was a solidly built, sound-proofed booth with a double-glass window into which all three cameras could be jammed side-by-side. When the director signaled his readiness to shoot, three operators stooped over and squeezed in beside them, the door was securely fastened, and the booth became an instant sauna. On the word "Cut," the door would burst open and three sweat-drenched camera operators would shoot out of the booth as though escaping a burning building. When the scene lasted more than a minute, an operator might be carried out in a faint. But somehow the work got done.

The art of photography had reached great heights in silent films, but literally overnight the invasion of sound forced it into a rather long period of retrogression. Set-ups were necessarily simplified, moving shots were nearly impossible to realize, and creative use of the lens was almost forgotten. Although the situation improved after the sound-proofed blimp elbowed the camera booth into history and a few directors liberated the camera for sequences void of dialogue, the dominance of the sound engineer and the natural reluctance to shake off newly acquired habits slowed the renascence of the art of motion pictures down to a slow crawl. Complete liberation from the strictures imposed by sound took more than a decade, but in the interim a few creative filmmakers continued their search for a way out of technology's maze. Understandably, there were a few blind alleys.

A few blind alleys and too many eyes. As soon as each camera could sport its own blimp, Edmund Goulding, making The Devil's Holiday *at Paramount, conceived an astonishing creation. He undertook to shoot a ten-minute-long scene with twenty-seven cameras, all running in sync, which in itself was no mean feat. The scene was staged in a three-room set, and the cameras were placed at appropriate vantage points outside its walls. Small holes were cut through the walls to accommodate the lenses, and paintings, drapes, and other decorations, each fitted with very fine lifting wires, were positioned over the openings. When the scene was shot the portholes in the walls serving as its background were covered by their wall decorations and presented a normal appearance, while the portholes through which cameras filmed the scene were cleared. As the action moved toward an adjacent wall or room, the porthole covers were manipulated accordingly. And so on, nearly ad infinitum.*

When a camera had served its purpose it could not be taken off the line without upsetting the entire system, so they all ran continuously, and each complete take exposed 27,000 feet of negative stock. There is no record of the number of takes made, but any scene running ten minutes is subject to error, and the probability of a satisfactory first take is close to zero. Which is why "Goulding's Folly" failed to gain entry into Hollywood's list of useful shots.

A few months later, in 1930, I was editing The Royal Family Of Broadway *at the Paramount Studio in Astoria, N.Y. Ina Claire and Frederic March co-starred, George Cukor and Cyril Gardner co-directed. The film was shot very much like the play it had been, and the three-camera technique was considered applicable. As was the custom, Camera A had a wide-angle lens to get the master, or establishing, shot; Camera B was fitted with a normal lens for close group or two shots. Camera C used a narrow-angle lens for the close-ups, and it was this camera Ina Claire, a very sharp lady, decided to favor.*

But it was not in that direction that she was always supposed to look, and directorial cunning had to deal with player sharpness. On some pretext, Camera D, accompanied by an operator and his assistant, was brought on the set and designated as the close-up camera. It was always placed where Claire (unaware that it was not loaded) could direct her reactions to both her and the directors' satisfaction. That very bright lady might have been deceived, or she may have quietly taken the hint, but from then on she played to Camera D.

CHAPTER SEVEN

Excepting plagiarists, forgers, and counterfeiters, most good artists find it difficult to cheat, and when it comes to making an honest living, art is a precarious line of work; the artist *must* depend on the whims and tastes of others. In Hollywood, that truth was never more evident than when the winds of change blew up a hurricane. Only the highest and the lowest echelons of the film industry were completely safe, and none of these was occupied by "artists," in the acceptable sense. Nearly all the top executives weathered the storm, as did most of the laborers and artisans. Craftsmen whose work changed little or not at all, such as set designers and camera personnel, felt hardly a breeze, but a Damoclean hatchet dangled on frazzled strings over the head of every writer, actor, and director in town. All at once, a talent for dialogue became a requirement in all these categories; actors with strong regional accents, grating voices, or a suspect tonal pitch were terminally handicapped; writers and directors with a tin ear for acceptable oral expression were unacceptable.

It was a time of fear and apprehension for the masters of a vanished art. Show-business veterans had always been aware that the public was fickle, and that profitable popularity was subject to sudden and often inexplicable reversal, but never had their own world turned on them in such a cold-blooded fashion.

The pain of termination, as in any beheading, comes not so much from the fall of the axe, but from the ineptitude with which the blow is delivered. In a closed community like Hollywood, ruled largely by chance, where a writer's block can last a lifetime, careers can collapse overnight; and where drugs and alcohol are used to relieve the stress and tensions that make ulcers the town's "occupational disease," the man who hires with pleasure is rarely a man who fires with pain. Since it is uncomfortable to wield the hatchet today on a friend or colleague of yesterday, that job is usually relegated to the artist's representative, or agent, and every successful "flesh peddler" develops a classic poker face as a form of self-immunization against any inclination to show feeling or compassion. Whether this is a psychological shield against the never-ceasing assaults on the agent's more tender sensibilities or an evolutionary trait that makes his occupation bearable has long been open to question, but sooner or later all of Hollywood's artists suffer the emotional trauma brought on by the sudden emergence of their agent's "fish-eyed" other self. Long before the artist-client senses the ice cold caress of an occupational ill wind, a chance encounter with his agent can announce misfortune. If his usually-hearty greeting, his firm handshake, and his eagerness to tell you his funny story of the day turn into a cold "Hi there…," a collapsing palm, and a hasty departure for a "Gosh, I almost forgot…" appointment, client beware! And if his eyes glaze as if curtained by a nictating membrane while they slip and shift, refusing to acknowledge your sudden look of alarm, it is a sure sign that more than your present job will soon be at stake; your whole career is sliding away like a tide-battered home in Malibu.

When your anxious calls are shunted off to a barricade of secretaries and assistants, it does not mean that your agent is cold and heartless—like the doctor who leaves the room where his patient is dying, the agent simply hates to see you suffer. And though an honest examination of the situation, however bleak, might ease the pain, it is rarely forthcoming—"The rest is silence." For hardly a single agent will alert his client to the truth, which he probably knows as well as anybody. And that, of course, leads to embarrassment and awkward moments, because some of the men and women who are considered failures do come back, as did a number of artists in the late '20s and early '30s who had been too quickly cast aside.

Famous Players' first all-talking motion picture, *Interference*, was ill-conceived and badly cast. Its only value was in uncovering more problems of change. Evelyn Brent, a silent star with a diamond-hard voice made harder by a strong Brooklyn accent, played the feminine lead, and Roy Pomeroy, the special-effects genius who had only his technical expertise to sustain him, directed. The result confirmed that technical proficiency alone was hardly enough; the "hardware" of the new medium had reached acceptability but the indispensable "wet ware" appeared to be in short supply. The producers' searching eyes turned toward New York and the Yale

School of the Theater, and it took no prophet to predict that the pendulum, having started its backward swing, would go too far.

Perhaps for the first time in its history, the westbound Super-Chief carried a heavier load than its eastbound twin. There was hope for the young of an over-crowded Broadway, and a challenge for those established stars who were willing to risk the contempt of their colleagues by exchanging the advantages of the superior snob status for a few weeks of sunshine and a few bags of gold; deserting Broadway for Hollywood was considered a rung back down the ladder. Nevertheless, actors like Walter Huston, Ruth Chatterton, Ina Claire, and Helen Hayes dared to sail into newly-charted seas. Of course, the Barrymores were immune to upturned noses, as were the Lunts—they had all served time in the silents. But other stage greats like Catherine Cornell insightfully refused to risk their hard-won eminence in a medium whose unbiased camera's eye might disclose a surplus of technique and a shortage of emotional honesty.

Those who led the new gold rush soon found that the time-honored techniques of the Broadway stage were out of place or downright counterproductive when practiced on a movie set. The theatrical posturings and gesticulations of a Bernhardt became material for second-rate clowns. The resonant voice which reached the balcony only shattered the much-closer sound valve; its overweening and bumptious tones were more fit for the melodramatic hero of an opera than a familiar on the movie screen, for the balcony had been brought down onto the playing ground where the microphone could make the honest whisper of "I love you" available to every ear. The affectations of the borrowed English accent, which Bill Wellman called "Kansas City British," was unacceptably pretentious to American film viewers, and broad facial and bodily reactions, dramatic on the stage, were just plain "hamming" on the screen. Perhaps the visiting actor's most startling discovery was that upstaging a fellow performer would get him nowhere; there was no "up" or "down," since the camera, the viewer's roving eye, operated in a field of 360 degrees on all three axes.[20]

In 1923 Douglas Fairbanks, Jr. was fourteen, and about to start his first silent picture, Stephen Steps Out. *Looking for another fourteen-year-old to play Doug's buddy, Joe Henabery, the director found Frankie Albertson working through the summer as a camera loader on the studio lot. Though completely inexperienced, he turned out to be a natural whose poise and relaxed manner made Doug Jr. look a bit stiff.*

A few years later Frank was out of high school and into a full-time screen career. When a well-known Broadway character actress was invited to test for an upcoming film, Frank was asked to play the scene with her. He was greatly impressed with the actress's name and her years of stage experience and he found it difficult to understand her obvious fear. Unable to remain silent, he took her trembling hands in his. "Honey," he said, "there's nothing to be afraid of. You have no audience to play to. When we shoot the scene, you just talk to me and I'll talk to you."

That was lesson number one in acting for the screen. She could build on that.

The introduction of stage directors was less felicitous than that of stage actors; it turned out to be more educational than beneficial. Most of the gold-seekers are forgotten but, apparently less concerned about their artistic standing than the actors, almost every director of note made the four-day trip to Hollywood at the behest of the studios.

In an industry that lays some claim to artistic endeavor, "logical thinking" is believed to separate the artist from the executive. Since the directors who had learned their craft in silent films were skilled in handling screen-oriented staging and set-ups, while their colleagues from the east were experts of the spoken word, the Hollywood producers reasoned that uniting the two special talents would add up to perfection—it worked with writers, didn't it? Unfortunately, the producers did not have G. B. Shaw's gift for spotting the alternative, and they overlooked the possibility that two half-wrongs plus two half-rights might add up to two disasters. They also overlooked the stubbornness of the ego.

Common sense should have warned them that two generals of equal rank can never lead an army to victory, a truism soon confirmed by the failure of the co-director concept. Like an unstable chemical compound, the teams soon came unstuck, leaving each director to make good on his own. To Hollywood's great surprise the silent directors adjusted to the demands of dialogue and sound more readily than the men of the theater adjusted to the use of filmic metaphor, the manipulation of the camera, and to limitless space. The immigrants were soon trekking back to New York while almost every silent director, except for those lost to normal attrition, survived the once-feared winds of change with little emotional shock.

However, a handful of stage directors were not only talented but adaptable, which is exactly what those who looked to the bell-shaped curve for their statistics on competence would have expected. The most successful of

Edward Dmytryk directing Guy Madison and Jean Porter (future Mrs. Dmytryk) in a scene for *'Til the End of Time*. 1945 or 46.

the lot was George Cukor, who made Hollywood his home. After a little more than a year as co-director with Cyril Gardner he was allowed to strike out on his own. His best films were adaptations of New York plays, but he quickly developed a knack for disguising their theatrical structure with a "movie look." John Cromwell shared director credit on two films with Eddie Sutherland, then soloed for some twenty years of moderately successful productions. When the pickings thinned out he made a successful return to Broadway. Rouben Mamoulian had a career in European and New York theaters behind him, but his first film, *Applause*, revealed a strongly creative approach to filmmaking which influenced many of Hollywood's directors. Unfortunately, conflicts with the brass hampered his career, and after ten years of challenging film work he spent most of his time in the theater. James Whale, an early import from the London stage, established a high standard for classic horror films with the *Frankenstein* series and *The Invisible Man*.

Some concepts concerning the failure of the majority of stage directors may be in order. They are matters of opinion, of course, but not necessarily inappropriate, since history is largely a mélange of perception and prejudice.

Assuming the presence of talent, such failures must have been the result of error or misjudgment on the part of the producers, the directors, or both, but the two most tenable explanations lie buried in a welter of misinformation. First, the producers erred through ignorance of the responsibilities of the creative personnel. The stage directors made the second mistake: a too-casual assumption that the intricacies of transition were slight, and largely in their favor.

The producers' mistake was to overestimate the need for experienced dialogue direction, a misconception still held by many students and scholars of the medium. The belief that it is necessary or advantageous to instruct actors in their handling of words is little short of ridiculous. An actor who must be coached to properly speak a line—any line—is not an actor. Unselfconscious, apparently spontaneous verbal expression (with its accompanying "body language") is a major part of a professional actor's skill,[21] and the director who understands the nuances of speech as well as Spencer Tracy did, or Jack Lemmon does, is rare indeed. Even Lord Olivier would not presume to mastermind a good actor's performance.

In any case, a silent director, baffled by dialogue, could not have gone far astray by trusting his actors. This was demonstrated by a few continental directors who were not at home with the English language or its American offshoot. Lubitsch, of course, was already a legend, but German director William Dieterle dumbfounded the skeptics with his first sound film, The Last Flight *(1930), in which the idiosyncrasies of American speech were essential. Although the cadence and inflections of the lines, written by John Monk Saunders in a rather special "Hemingway" style, were completely foreign to Dieterle, they were skillfully handled by an American cast headed by Richard Barthelmess, a silent star of long standing though with little stage training.*

The second mistake was made by most of the theater directors who discounted the aesthetic differences of stage and screen, especially as they related to audience awareness and acceptance. Surprisingly, lack of editing, camera, or set-up expertise presented few problems. Although camera placement was (and still is) the total responsibility of a competent filmmaker, it has always been routine for the inexperienced director to use either the cinematographer or the editor to help in the selection of the set-ups necessary to cover a scene. This is exactly what Cukor did throughout a long and eminently successful career. But Cukor did understand film pace.

Pace was the obstacle that tripped up almost all stage directors. It is extremely difficult for even the most experienced actors to objectively gauge the difference between the pace of a scene played live on the set and the appearance of that pace as it will play to the viewer watching it on the screen. Every good director is extremely aware of pace, consciously or unconsciously, and he controls it accordingly. In a discussion of tempo with a well-known film and TV director, I mentioned my discovery of speed ratio while I was a projectionist. His eyes lit up. "That's it!" he almost shouted. "I knew film action required more speed, but I never knew why. That explains it." Of course, that was a confirmation, not an explanation, which is still somewhat hypothetical. But it was an unfortunate fact that even men like George Abbott, whose theatrical productions seemed to move swiftly, failed to realize that live movement and screen movement vary widely in their impact on the viewer. His few films moved so deliberately that the audience was mired in a bog of boredom. And Abbot was by no means alone.

To sum it all up, by 1931 the winds of change had become whispering zephyrs, and though much had been moved about little had been uprooted. The storm's most damaging blasts had forced retreat and retrenchment in once-established areas, and the only unique contribution to the heterogeneous art of the cinema, the montage, which had been so skillfully developed by the Russians, suffered a blow from which it has not yet recovered. Optimum manipulation of the camera, both from the directors' and the photographers' points of view, was sidetracked for years; but the lens was still a lens, film was slowly improving in quality, and the complete recovery of the art of photography was only a matter of time. Furthermore, the demands of embryonic sound, which had boxed in the directors, only forced them to greater effort not to re-invent, but to redesign the movie "wheel."

Fortunately, that responsibility was in the hands of those who had perfected the original model. Frank Capra, Jack Ford, George Stevens, Leo McCarey, William Wyler, King Vidor, Frank Borzage, Sam Wood, and, of course, Raoul Walsh, a leading man who became a leading director when he lost an eye in an accident, were all survivors from the silent era, and all were benignly imprinted by action films disguised as comedies and westerns. They dominated the '30s and '40s, and it was two full decades after the inception of dialogue before a veteran of the New York stage, Elia Kazan, won an Academy Award.

When the screen began to talk the flowering of a great pictorial art was nipped in mid-bloom. Led by the emotional resistance of Charlie Chaplin, who realized he had everything to lose and nothing to gain, a few of Hollywood's creative colony fought a hopeless battle, but the industry as a whole saw the revolution as a highly profitable transition rather than the death of a dynamic art form, and they greeted it with enthusi-

Edward Dmytryk with John Wayne. *Back to Bataan*, 1944.

asm. However, that response was subdued in the acting community; its greatest problem was the introduction of dialogue. There were no film criteria with which to measure the quality of the talking, either as scripted or as spoken. The only established norms were those of the live theater, many of whose rules and conventions were hoary with age, and all the actors, whether from the stage or from silent films, unwittingly abided by them. Although the huge film audience was not as sophisticated nor as literate as the theater's silk-stocking crowd, it quickly noticed and as quickly rejected a style of speech and reaction which, when projected on a great screen, was magnified and exaggerated into caricature and grandiloquence.

The wiser actors soon developed techniques to fit the historically new medium, but artistic pretensions accumulated over the course of many decades are hard to recognize and admit, let alone modify, and the degree of modification often failed to please. It took a number of years for actors trained in the theater to recognize that honesty of characterization was more important than melodramatic effect.

This story, which is not apocryphal, is an oft-told tale that, in the context of the development of film acting as a distinct skill, should be repeated here.

Jack Lemmon was twenty-nine, and acting in his first motion picture, It Should Happen To You. *George Cukor had nearly twenty-five years of studio experience and was a master of film acting techniques. After the first scene rehearsal Cukor suggested that Jack "bring it down a little." Lemmon, fresh from the theater, brought it down, but hardly enough, and Cukor repeated his request. This de-escalation continued for several rehearsals until, in utter desperation, Lemmon blurted out, "But Mr. Cukor! You don't want me to act at all!"*

"That's the idea, dear boy," said George. "That's the idea."

That oversimplification was given legitimacy by Olivier's half-serious remark that the essence of screen acting is "not to act at all." In equally simplistic terms other actors, like John Wayne, have said, "I don't act, I react." A third, somewhat deceptive assessment, which is more profound than it seems, holds that in films, one doesn't "act," one "is."

These maxims, or opinions, are not meant to challenge the "tea-party" teaching principles of America's thousands of acting schools, almost all of which still preach the gospel of the theater, but to emphasize the technical and philosophical differences that had to be reconciled when the stage invaded the studio set. After a period of trial and error many of the good stagetrained actors managed the transition with skill. Most silent actors, however, found it more a problem of discovery than of transition. And though the former outnumbered the latter from the start, film actors like Gary Cooper, John Wayne, Elizabeth Taylor, and Mary Astor held their own with stage actors such as Ruth Chatterton, Frederic March, Walter Huston, and Spencer Tracy.

A reminiscence from the horse's mouth. In 1930 Spencer Tracy abandoned a Broadway career for Hollywood, where he made such a successful switch to film that by the middle '30s he was known as "The Prince of Underplayers." In 1938 he won a second Oscar for his performance in Boys Town. *His co-star in the film was Mickey Rooney, famous for his energy and flamboyance after eleven years of studio work. However, during their first scene together he spoke his lines in such a controlled whisper that Tracy was baffled. Never one to hide his reactions to what he considered professional misbehavior, he stopped in mid-take. "Hey, kid," he growled. "Why are you whispering like that?"*

"Mr. Tracy," replied Mickey in normal tones, "I was told that you under-played everything, and the only way I could top you was to speak more quietly than you do."

"Hell! I can shout as loud as anyone when the situation demands it," roared Tracy. "And if you keep whispering we'll have one of those situations right now!"

That was probably the last time an actor tried to finesse Spencer Tracy.

In several years of cross-breeding the studios amassed a pool of actors as famous for its quality as for its size. With the possible exception of England, where actors take a little longer to shuck their dramatic school techniques, no other country can match Hollywood for talent.

I was in London to make a film and a member of the cast caught my attention.

"You make films in Hollywood," he said. "You're very lucky."

I was about to agree with him, but my curiosity was aroused. "Why?" I asked.

"Because you have so many wonderful actors out there," he said.

Quick dissolve to Hollywood—a few weeks later. A colleague stopped me to say hello.

"I hear you've been shooting in England." I nodded.

"You're lucky," he said.

"Why?"

"Because they have so many wonderful actors over there."

Show people are sometimes considered an odd lot, but no other group of artists views honest talent with so much respect and so little jealousy.

CHAPTER EIGHT

Change powerful enough to stimulate a renaissance reached even those recesses that rarely catch the historian's eye. There, like the first warm breeze of spring, it nudged hibernating aspirations into wakefulness. All at once, a career in films seemed more attractive than life as a teacher of mathematics and, as I looked around the campus and compared it to the lot, certainly more exciting. I dropped out of Cal-Tech and put my name on the cutting department's waiting list, but not before recruiting some friends of my own age out of the mail room and into the projection booths. (From there two of them emerged as first-class film editors, and the third as an independent producer.)

A friend's intercession could get one inside a studio gate, but the nature of the more creative crafts allowed only those with ability to stay there. Of course there was a certain amount of nepotism in the executive ranks, but it was not as extensive as some sour-grapes criers would have one believe. And, as a rule, the family-favored were ensconced in positions that hardly hindered the advancement of the unrelated. At MGM it was slyly rumored that all north-facing offices in the executive building were occupied by relatives whose duty it was to keep a sharp eye out for glaciers of the next ice age. On the other hand, relatives with talent were an occasional possibility. William Wyler, one of Hollywood's truly great directors, was a distant nephew of Carl Laemmle, the head of Universal Studio. Yet he started in silents as an apprentice prop man then worked his way through several other categories before he earned a director's chair.

In the western world apprenticeship is an abandoned tradition.[22] But it is still the best way to discover and develop nascent talents, whether they favor the crafting of a fine pair of shoes, the building of a cathedral, or the creation of an exceptional motion picture. Happily, the studios initiated perhaps the most effective on-the-job training of their time. The theory behind it went like this: if enough people pull enough levers on enough one-arm bandits, sooner or later someone will hit the jackpot. And if enough young men and women are put under contract, coached, and tested as craft assistants or by playing bits, parts, or feature roles in films, sooner or later a new star will shine in Hollywood's sky.

Star! There was a time when that word meant something to those who strove for recognition in the field of entertainment, and to the millions who were entertained. It was a significant part of the luster of the Golden Age. To Frank Capra, and to the rest of us, it meant your name above *the title—just think about that. It meant the actor was "distinguished above all others in quality, rank, etc." Now it has no more significance than the adjective "Jumbo," when applied to olives or eggs, and it is often awarded, as are many high-falutin' titles, in exchange for a cut in salary. Labeling an actor a "star" has never made one.*

A part of the Hollywood myth contends that in its heyday there were more young actors of superlative talent parading Hollywood Boulevard than ever graced the screen as stars. That was clearly an instance of the everyday regurgitation of Aesop's "Fox and Grapes." In the movies, where face, body, talent, intelligence, and an unexplainable aura are equal parts of the recipe for stardom, the absence of one or more of these ingredients does not necessarily doom a thespian to failure, but it does relegate him or her to a lesser category. However, the last ingredient is indispensable, and early in my life I was granted an insight into this mystery. In compliance with the best cinematic technique it was an incident without dialogue.

Walking along a studio street one day, I became aware of an attractive girl coming in my direction. Of course, I thought—the flaming red hair, the pouting lips, the flashy figure—Clara Bow! Paramount's brightest star of the Roaring Twenties. But as she walked by, I was not so sure; something seemed to be missing.[23] Still, with nothing to lose, I decided that I had seen the "It" girl in person.

A few days later I saw her again, but this time there was no room for doubt. The same look that had graced what I now realized must have been her stand-in was there, but magnified a hundred-fold by the added factor of a film personality that, as always, was indescribable. Today they say of such a star, "The camera loves her," and that probably says it better than any psychological analysis.

With a fresh influx of talent from all parts of the country, the studios put their jackpot theory to the test. It seemed that everyone got his or her chance. Bevies of young actors categorized as "stock girls" and "stock boys" were signed to seven-year contracts, with six-month options for the studios. Large pools of junior writers were recruited on the strength of their abilities as displayed in the numerous magazines of the '30s that featured their short stories. The directors' pool was already in place—any good editor who showed traces of a directing personality was sure of a B film as a test of his talent and a few of them "cut it."[24]

The junior writers benefited from their interaction with another pool, the studios' star system. They wrote to order. Example: at Paramount each star could make two or more films a year, and scripts were selected or written to fit their screen personalities. A number of young writers, usually working in teams of two, would be assigned to develop stories for, let us say, Carole Lombard's screen persona. If any of the scripts showed possibilities, some senior writer like Claude Binyon or Charles Brackett would polish it into a shootable film vehicle. If a junior writer turned out more hits than misses, he made senior rank. Those who didn't were eventually replaced by fresh talent which took its turn at running the gauntlet. For the pool system was, of course, a filter which winnowed out those who, for one reason or another, couldn't quite make it. Naturally, the fallout was extremely high and totally unpredictable.

One year Paramount proudly corralled the ten leading graduates of the Yale School of the Theater. Within two years all had disappeared except one man who managed to hang in for a few years as the editor of the studio trivia monthly.

Changes in Hollywood's creative fields were matched by changes in the studios' physical plants. The new stages had little in common with the flimsy barns of the silent era. They required new structural techniques and new materials from bottom to top. Their walls were a full four feet thick, with most of the space devoted to soundproofing; their padded doors, suspended on runners, were two stories tall to permit the passage of pre-assembled sections of sets; their ceilings were eighteen to twenty feet high to accommodate the construction of scaffolds, or gantries, for overhead lamps. Their foundations had to be strong enough to support this tremendous poundage, while their walls had to hold up the expansive ceilings over floors free of columns to facilitate the movement of cameras and sets. Unchanged for the last sixty years, they have remained Hollywood landmarks and testaments to the skills of their designers and builders. In an era when every state-of-the-art development has a follow-up already on the boards, they remain invulnerable. In all probability, they will be here sixty years from now.

Paramount's first sound complex was a block of four connected stages and their adjoining recording rooms. (The speed of development soon rendered these huge rooms obsolete by providing small on-stage, recording booths.) The first sets built on one of these stages was dressed and waiting for Dorothy Arzner's call to "action." Dorothy, who had been a cutter when I was on the Sunset lot, was following in the footsteps of Lois Weber, America's first successful woman director. Arzner's career was beginning as Weber's was nearing its end. She was to start shooting on Monday, but on the preceding Saturday fate rearranged her schedule.

Darkness was settling down on the lot and workers were heading for "home and mother" when a small fire, sparked by a short-circuit flickered into life in one of the stage walls. Unfortunately, the wall's soundproofing was flammable and, since the stage had been abandoned for the day, the blaze had acquired size and strength before it was discovered.

Cutters and their assistants often work late, and several of us were still at our movieolas. However, the first alarm sent us clambering up the stairs to the roof of our building, which was some 200 feet from the burning stage. We watched the unfolding drama as smoke turned into tongues of flame, then the first screaming fire engines raced through the studio gates and the firefighters began a long night's work. What followed was a true spectacular, as mesmerizing as it was frightening. By the time the firemen had strung out their hoses and turned on the water the flat roof of the nearest stage was writhing in agony, convulsively rolling out in a series of waves like swells on a wind-lashed sea. The firefighters had placed a ladder against the stage and two of them had climbed to the roof to hose it down, but the undulating surface made their positions untenable and they headed for the ground and safety.

It was undoubtedly the department's first experience with this type of con-

struction, and they had planted the ladder in front of the huge stage doors. *The two firemen were halfway down when the double doors blew open as if propelled by a full charge of TNT. Like two bags of soiled laundry the men were launched into space.*

One of the men was killed, the other severely injured. It was some time before Arzner started shooting her make-believe drama.

A gentler, kindler lightning struck twice in 1929.

First, a Cal-Tech background, skimpy though it was, facilitated my move from the projection booth to a cutting cubicle and an assistant cutter's job.

Those were the good old days. Women were considered delicate and incapable of handling any mechanism more complicated than a Singer sewing machine. In the opinion of some executives, that made them incompetent to deal with the mechanization of the sound-cutting process. During the first two years of sound, all but one woman editor left the Paramount lot. They were replaced by men. In time, the arrival of the numbering machine freed film from the synchronizer and made such reasoning moot. It was also reluctantly admitted that women were at least as deft as men, and anyway, talent, which was asexual, mattered more than digital dexterity. Slowly, chauvinism vacated the scene—at least in the cutting rooms.

Second, four years of high school Spanish and the absence of unions and their seniority systems slid me into a position as editor of Spanish-language films within a matter of months. Those films were a brief but interesting footnote in the story of sound—they were also sad examples of trying to outguess the state-of-the-art.

With the demise of silents Hollywood was in danger of losing its world market. The substitution of foreign translations for English titles had been a simple process; the substitution of dozens of foreign languages for American dialogue was a much more complicated procedure for which, at the moment, there was no quick fix. The studios marked time while the experts worked on the problem, but in the interim two expedients were tried.

The first was a denial of established editorial dogma, a perverse cutting technique that pleased only the avant-gardist or the "reacting" actor. Seeing actors speak their lines was avoided by playing those lines over cuts of the listeners. This enabled translators to replace American dialogue without resorting to lip-synching, a technique still too crude to please the viewer.[25]   (If the experiment had been continued, it might have led to a filmmaking genre that relied more on metaphor and image than on speech—"a consummation devoutly to be wished.")

The first expedient worked briefly in Europe and Asia, but Paramount considered the Spanish-speaking world sufficiently large and profitable to merit a second expedient, even though it was far more costly. It entailed a complete reshooting of an English-language film with a Spanish-speaking cast. The original sets were retained, and many of the original crew, as well as the director (whether or not he was at home with the language) reprised their roles in the production of the Spanish-speaking film.

The English version of *Grumpy*, one of Paul Lucas' earliest Hollywood films, was co-directed by Cyril Gardner and George Cukor, but an American dialogue expert was hardly needed on the Spanish, *El Grunidor*, so Gardner directed this version alone. It was decided, however, that the editor, at least, should understand what was being said, by whom, to whom, and when. As fate would have it, I was the only person within reach who had a working knowledge of Spanish and so, to my great surprise, I was suddenly a full editor.

At first blush it seemed an ingenious idea, a creative stratagem for saving, even strengthening, the market. The Spanish-speaking stars cost a good deal less that their English-speaking predecessors, so no expense was spared to buy the best talent available. One of Spain's top theatrical stars, a Senor Vilches, was imported to play the title role. The supporting players were home-market favorites from Mexico, Argentina, Peru, Colombia—wherever. Together this all-star cast, which was expected to please the Spanish-speaking world no end, scuttled Paramount's ship of goodwill.

Hollywood filmmakers had already learned that American viewers had an aversion to the affectations of Oxford University or West End speech, but they had completely overlooked the fact that the number of dialects and accents in the Spanish-speaking countries of the world was, for all practical purposes, nearly unlimited. The Spaniards and the punctilious Colombians found it difficult to understand the Cuban's clipped, rapid-fire speech—besides, they hated the sound of it. The Argentineans considered the musical cadences of the Mexicans a bit discordant, while the Mexicans cared even less for the harsh Argentinean pronunciations. And so it went, as Anna's king would say, "Et cetera, et cetera, et cetera!"

Nobody was happy. Although a second Spanish-language feature was filmed before the first was released, that ended the experiment. Fortunately, it was not too long before looping and dubbing facilities were established in all the world's film centers. Until then, superimposed titles served as an unaffected surrogate for speech as, to some extent, they still do today.

Although modern looping is quite successful, it has its drawbacks, drawbacks of which most people are unaware. I was reminded by co-workers in Rome that most Italians have never heard Spencer Tracy speak, nor Bogart, Gable, Garbo, Brando, or any of Hollywood's greats. Their voices are replaced by the lip-synched voices of Italian actors, some of whom "ghost-speak" for several different Hollywood stars. The resulting similarities in vocalization must have many Italians (and French, and Germans, and other non-Americans, as they listen to their own language versions) wondering at the extent to which our actors ape each other's vocal singularities. But those Europeans who insist on the genuine article attend the few large-city theaters that run films in the original tongues. Even if some of them don't totally understand the "lyrics" they relish the "tunes."

CHAPTER NINE

"Chaos often breeds life," wrote Henry Adams, and it is true that in the absence of certainty and stability the gates of opportunity yawn wide for the fortunate few who question the rules and quarrel with orthodoxy. Inevitably the desk jockeys will make new rules out of the creators' breakthroughs, but for a time, at least, the rule-breakers know true excitement and occasional rapture; no drug can match the high of the birthing of an original idea.

To a considerable extent '28 and '29 were years of chaos in the film world. The artistry developed in the silent era was drowning in a sea of decibels, phones, and background noise. On the eve of its establishment as a true cinematic art, montage sank into oblivion, sound was king, and to hell with "the picture worth a thousand words."

But sound was also a catalyst, for the tighter the bonds the greater the effort to break free. Experiment and invention were the order of the day. For those who welcomed a dare, spring was always in the air; even the Cal-Tech graduates who invaded the movie lots with their United Rubber Handbooks and their bags of electronic tricks had a light in their eyes and a buoyancy in their step I had never seen on the campus. They too were responding to the challenge of the new field; their Xs and Ys now stood for unknowns of a different order whose unriddling would lead to more unknowns beyond, in a neverending game of hide-and-seek.

Beyond the concern with dialogue, the creating, recording and editing of sound effects, which had a low priority indeed, became a fertile field for free-wheeling ingenuity.

One day, ever-curious, I walked into the just-completed music stage. In one lonely corner of the vast chamber, designed to accommodate a full philharmonic orchestra, sat a small man amid a small truckload of instruments. Surrounded by what seemed to be a random pile of drums, cymbals, and other paraphernalia, he was creating sound effects for a Western. Fascinated, I listened as he matched the hoof beats of the horses on the screen by clopping a pair of what looked like halves of a coconut shell. His name was Mr. Brown, and he was doing exactly what he had been doing for years at New York's Paramount Theater while accompanying silent films.

Some time later he faked the sound of bacon frying by rustling a sheet of cellophane. Cellophane? Why not the genuine article? Because bacon frying does not record realistically, explained the mixer, and I wondered what effect would best suggest the rustling of a sheet of cellophane.

A few years later the sound of Roman arrows puncturing Christian flesh in DeMille's Sign Of The Cross *was simulated by hitting a slack ukulele string with a drumstick. Now* that *was creativity.*

Almost overnight a potential art form became a mongrel, a mixture of art, electronics, and machinery. With its two partners not yet housebroken, art had to sweat it out. As for the holdovers, the projectionists, photographers, actors, and directors were not the only film workers subjected to revolutionary changes; the film editors had even more difficult problems to solve. In the absence of numbering machines they jury-rigged systems for maintaining sync without the use of synchronizers, which minimized time-wasting manipulation that added nothing to the art of editing. In the absence of sound movieolas methods were improvised for locating sounds and syllables with a black grease pencil and the aid of a patient projectionist. Naturally, the improvisations varied from the ingenious to the unworkable, and the responsibility for the problem-solving fell mainly on the members of a new category that had sidled into the picture with sound—the assistant cutters.

Anne Bauchens was a quiet, spinsterish woman, which was not surprising; she was also DeMille's editor, one of the members of his retinue who took seriously his demand for total veneration. Her mind was as set as her marcelled gray hair and, like Charlie Chaplin, she found it difficult to come to terms with the existence and the intricacies of the expanded medium. Before the sound movieola was manufactured in quantities sufficient to accommodate all of Hollywood's editors, most of us were ferreting out ways to effectuate the "reading" of sound.

Universal Studios, 1931

Anne rejected innovations.[26] Instead, her assistant, a tall, rangy young man named Everett, was asked to write all the dialogue in each scene on the clear half of the film strip that carried the sound track, and write it exactly where it occurred.

Since DeMille usually shot at least two thousand feet of film each day, most of which contained dialogue, Everett required more time to transcribe the spoken lines than C. B. took to shoot them. Everett's forbearance and his dogged determination to let nothing dim his desire to cut film despite the unreasonable demands made at that stage of his apprenticeship was wonderful to see. For even when sound movieolas were available to all, Anne's was used primarily to facilitate Everett's laborious transcriptions.

In the absence of sound movieolas the laboratories moved quickly to aid the editors in their efforts to domesticate sound. Earlier, each picture had occupied the full width of the 35mm film between the sprocket holes. Now, in printing, the picture's size was diminished to accommodate a clear, transparent strip, approximately 3/16 of an inch wide, along the picture's left edge. This corresponded to the width of the sound track which was photographically deposited on a separate strip of otherwise transparent 35mm film. When the picture strip was placed over its matching track a slight readjustment of the movieola's film gate permitted the doubled film to be viewed as one, with the sound's striations fully visible through the picture's overlying clear strip. Now a facility for decoding the striations, an ability to read the actor's lips, and the script notes, which recorded the dialogue as shot whether or not it followed the scene as written, enabled a mentally agile cutter to "read" the scene without ever hearing the words.

It was a puzzle-solver's delight; I fell in love with the system. I have always believed the term "moving pictures," defines the medium, that it unequivocally underscores the overriding importance of the moving image, and that the editing of such images into skillfully conceived juxtaposition has a preponderant role in the construction and final appeal of a well-made motion picture.[27]

Throughout my years as a cutter I did all my cutting on a silent movieola. Later, as a director always involved in the hands-on cutting of my films, I did most of my work on the disconnected picture head of a sound movieola. The reasoning was simple; the best way to cut a picture is to cut the picture.

Before leaving the silent era altogether it is only proper to intone a requiem for the virtually abandoned film art of opposition, apposition, and contiguity: the montage. In Europe that word is applied to editing in general; in Hollywood it is reserved for the construction of a series of cuts largely, if not altogether, sans dialogue, which strive to involve the viewer in determinable emotions. That definition will make little sense to those not completely familiar with the potential of creative editing, and "those" includes many people who have spent their lives in the studios, not excepting a number of working cutters. Perhaps a simple example will enlighten the reader.

Two of Russia's early filmmakers, Pudovkin and Kuleshov, concocted a classic experiment. They shot a single close-up of the actor Mosjykhine, whose face was set in a completely neutral expression. Printing three copies of the take, they intercut them with (1) a close shot of a plate of soup, (2) a shot of a dead woman in a coffin, and (3) a close shot of a little girl playing with a toy. What followed is best told in Pudovkin's words.

"When we showed the three combinations to an audience which had not been let into the secret...(they) raved about the acting of the artist. They pointed out the heavy pensiveness of his mood over the forgotten soup, were moved by the deep sorrow with which he looked at the dead woman, and admired the light, happy smile with which he surveyed the girl at play. But

we knew that in all these cases the face was exactly the same." (Film Techniques, V. I. Pudovkin.)

That ingenious demonstration was the beginning of a second-level development in the art of filmmaking, a movement soon blocked by the eruption of sound. But sound has been successfully absorbed into filmmaking for many years now, and there is no excuse for the continuing neglect of montage, the *only* original art in the medium. Sadly, it will continue in limbo as long as most cutters' efforts are totally expended on the registration of reality alone. As all good artists know, reality is to art as a cadaver is to a living, breathing member of the human race.

I have leaned on editors beyond their just desserts. Without question an occasional film is saved, or even made, by a virtuosic editor (if the necessary material has been supplied by the director), but many, many more are damaged by careless or incompetent hacking. The fault, of course, lies with their superiors, both directors and executives, who have never learned the finer points of editing, and therefore have no reasonable basis for intelligent appraisal of the cutters' work. A further road-block to good cutting, largely in the television field, is the demand for the final cut "by the end of the week," which leaves little time for properly finishing, let alone finessing, the editor's work. However, the greatest fiascos result when inexperienced directors or, occasionally, "power" actors insist on final creative control. That is the equivalent of a fry-cook demanding the right to prepare a four-star feast.

CHAPTER TEN

It is comforting to think that in the early days of Hollywood there may have been near parity in the tug-of-war between business and art, but by the '60s, when the conglomerates took advantage of the market and snapped up the studios, art was a gone goose. In 1966, Gulf and Western Industries claimed Paramount as its slice of the Hollywood pie.

Not long after that takeover I was a guest at a small dinner in Rome given in honor of Gulf and Western's chairman, Mr. Charles Bludhorn, who had made a fortune in sewing machines. On that occasion only one memory occupies a permanent cubbyhole in my mind. At one point in our conversation Bludhorn, a complete newcomer to filmmaking, opined, "One year from now I will know more about the movies than anyone in Hollywood." Nobody laughed.

This temporary leap in time was made to pinpoint an inherent problem in the generally twitchy partnership of art and industry, a sticky wicket that has always been with us. Whatever their educational or occupational backgrounds, most studio executives become "artists" in a remarkably short time after taking office. Like a family birthright, a "feeling" for the medium, which most gifted actors, writers, editors, cinematographers, and directors take years to develop, apparently comes with the job. As can be expected, instant indoctrination and hard experience rarely find common ground.

I have known few executives as openly hubristic as Bludhorn, and many who were downright decent and not spooked by self-doubt, but in between...My first brush with "unquestionable authority" saddled me with a psychic allergy that for many years brought on a painful "rash" every time I faced presumptuous privilege.

By the time I was transferred to Paramount's Marathon Avenue lot in late '27 or early '28, B. P. Schulberg was the studio head. The lot's few intellectuals dubbed him The Gray Eminence, not because of any diplomatic brilliance but because of his livid complexion and his dour personality. I had noticed his complexion in passing, but my first contact with his persona was at an editorial running of *Close Harmony*, a film co-directed by Eddie Sutherland and John Cromwell. It was a light musical comedy starring Nancy Carroll and Buddy Rogers, which gave me no cause for apprehension. (I was the assistant cutter on the film.)

He stalked into the studio's main theater accompanied by his henchmen, each of whom held an executive position on the lot and was considered a "wheel." Without any preliminary chatter, which should have been a giveaway, the group was seated, the house lights were doused, and the film was started. I waited for the film's first laugh, but when the scene played there was not a titter. And it got worse. Not once during the running did B. P. laugh or even twist his blue lips into the semblance of a smile. And when one of his toadies started to chuckle at an undeniably funny line, Schulberg glanced back at him in disapproval, and the man nearly choked in his effort to abort his instinctive reaction.

I knew every cut in the film, so I spent most of the running covertly watching B. P.'s yes-men, lit by the dim, flickering light reflected from the screen, as they fought to suppress spontaneous laughter. I realized then why they had all seated themselves well behind their boss; they didn't dare sit where their emotional struggles could be seen. They had neither courage nor pride, and B. P. hated comedy.

At about that time Leo McCarey, after a highly successful start as a writer, director, and producer for Hal Roach and the team of Laurel and Hardy, was hired to make one of his first full-length features for Paramount. He was still shooting when Schulberg assumed his duties as First Vice-President in charge of production. After viewing some of Leo's dailies he wasted no time, or tact, in expressing his feelings about comedy as a genre and McCarey as a director.[28] But not until five or six years later, after B. P. had been fired and Leo was back on the lot did I hear the denouement from McCarey's own lips.

In 1934 I was cutting *Ruggles Of Red Gap* for McCarey and, pursuant to the practice at Paramount, I was with him on the set. As was his wont, Leo was noodling on the ever-present piano while the set was being lit. In time his assistant arrived to announce, "All is ready, sir." Leo nodded absent-mindedly

Renoir's *Grand Illusion*, 1937.

and continued playing. The assistant retired politely, but in twenty minutes he was back. His announcement was somewhat stronger, but McCarey's reaction was the same. The assistant looked toward me for help, but we had been through this routine before, and I shrugged my shoulders. I was sure Leo had heard and understood. Defeated once more, the assistant withdrew, only to return ten minutes later with a firmer step and a louder voice. With so much idle time the crew was beginning to get out of hand, and the assistant's "We're ready, Leo!" was much more urgent.

This time Leo shook his head as if waking from a reverie, and turned to his aide. "Oh, I'm sorry," he said. "I didn't hear you. I'll be right there."

As the assistant left to alert the crew, Leo winked at me and smiled. Then, by way of explanation, he flashed back some five or six years.

"On the last day of shooting Let's Go Native," *he said, "Paramount's paymaster visited my set. As I said, 'Cut, and print it!' on the final scene he handed me my closing check.*

I picked up my coat and headed straight for the front gate, which I refused to re-enter until that blue-lipped son-of-a-bitch was off the lot." The rest was a sort of confession.

"I can't forget, and I won't forgive," he said. "Every time I work at Paramount I still feel Schulberg's presence, and there's only one way I can shake the mood. I squander enough time to cost the studio a couple of hundred thousand bucks. It gives me a great deal of satisfaction."

Anyone who thinks such behavior is rare should think again—and again and again. It happens much more often than most executives realize. At times it is a subconscious act of revenge; more often it is a willful act of reprisal, of "getting mine back."

Members of three categories are the chief recipients of actual, or imagined, slights or indignities at the hands of someone in power; they are also in the best positions to exact satisfaction without danger of discovery, if they so desire. Who can tell whether a writer, earning a salary he considers inadequate, is really having a writer's block or just extending his working time (and weekly salary)? Who can be sure an actor, seething at some insult or injury, is not purposely stalling when he seems to be having trouble with his lines, his business, his memory, or hitting his marks? And who can tell whether a director is truly having difficulty in blocking out a complicated scene, honestly wooing his muse or, like Leo McCarey, just savoring his revenge for humiliation inflicted by a man who has long since hit the skids? I would venture to say that since the advent of sound a billion dollars have gone down the drain just in getting even.

Some executives are aware of the possibilities and take great care in their treatment of artists, who are the swiftest to feel hurt and the most likely to retaliate. But many more are insensible to the backlash of a sensitive worker for what he considers mistreatment. And a few just don't care.

In simplistic but not unreal terms it can be said that artists often provoke an adversarial situation, not only with those who pay them their huge salaries, but with other artists. This is especially true in show business. Since artists, way down deep, are characteristically insecure about the quality or appeal of their work, they are inclined to be overprotective of their opinions—after all, in a field where standards are subject to attack, whose fancy is more important, yours or mine? The possibility of an open conflict between writer and director, between director and actor, and especially between any of these three and the producer, the top executive, or almost any representative of the company's financial interests, is almost always present. The director who demands the right to produce his films is not really anxious to assume additional responsibilities or trying to be an "auteur"; he is actually simplifying his work in reducing by one the number of "visions" he will have to deal with during the film's production.

While it is true that most film artists prefer to dodge confrontation by using their agents as go-betweens (which is why the Lord created them), not all uncomfortable situations are that easily avoided. Some of these inescapable episodes were amusing but others were quite violent.

The producer of Ruggles was Arthur Hornblow, whose total filmography is quite impressive. But in 1934 his experience as a producer was rather meager, and hardly up to working with a man of McCarey's talent or temperament. Leo, my favorite director, was a man to approach guardedly during production.[29] *He often asked for reactions and ideas, which he would mull over for a possible germ, but he was a cold and quick death to anyone who, like Hornblow, thought it was his duty to insist on uninvited "input." The producer's daily set visits were a trial to Leo, who always ad-libbed his rehearsals regardless of the script, even when he was the co-writer. Such a weird and wonderfully creative mind was a mystery beyond Hornblow's more prosaic understanding.*

One day, after viewing the day's rushes, which McCarey had not yet seen, Hornblow invaded the set with comments. (He was the type of executive who took good work for granted and commented only on what he considered inferior.) His dissection of the scenes was too much for Leo, whose attention was on the job at hand, and he suggested that Hornblow return to his lair. Fueled by misplaced dignity, Hornblow drew himself up to his imagined height and refused to leave the stage. McCarey signaled two grips who had been standing nearby; they picked up the producer, whose protests went unheeded, and heaved him out the stage door.

Leo, for his part, sat down at the piano and spent a half hour recovering his cool—and punishing Paramount.

I led a relatively blissful film life; none of my associations with producers were that physical (though one came close) and most were quite compatible. As for emotional or artistic confrontations, which will occur, a director can do no better than follow in the footsteps of that master of suavity, Howard Hawks.

Hawks would greet a concerned producer with great courtesy, call for another director's chair, and seat the visitor at his side. He would lead the conversation into a discussion of the day's events, of the latest happenings in the sports arenas, or of any subject outside the work in progress. After ten or fifteen minutes of chit-chat the producer would glance around the set, discover that cast and crew had all slipped out for coffee or Cokes, and realize that as long as he was on the stage no work would be done. His hasty departure was usually assured.

Of course, some producers were made of sterner stuff, but Hawks had a solution for any situation.

In a pre-production discussion of one of his Columbia films, Hawks and Harry Cohn had apparently agreed on a specific treatment of a certain sequence. However, when it was filmed, Hawks changed his mind, and most probably improved the original concept. Such a reconstruction is not infrequent in the work of any good director.

The next day Cohn saw the rushes and flew into one of his well-catalogued rages. He stormed onto the set, accused Howard of breaking his word, and demanded that the sequence be reshot as originally conceived. To everybody's surprise, Hawks calmly agreed.

The following day he reshot the sequence—word for word and set-up for set-up as he had shot it two days before. Once more Cohn saw the dailies, rushed to the set in even higher dudgeon, and repeated his demand. And once more Howard acquiesced. But once more the retakes were duplicates of the first and second day's shooting.

There is no record of Cohn's reaction on seeing the latest rushes, but he was too smart to make the same mistake three times running. Irresistible force had met immovable object head on and had surrendered. His only remaining resort was to fire Hawks, but though Harry Cohn may have been rash, he was not a fool.

Chapter Eleven

Webster's leanest definition of 'boulevard' is "A broad, handsome avenue in a city." In 1929 Hollywood was not yet a city, and Hollywood Boulevard was not very broad and anything but handsome (the penchant for assuming a fancy "handle" in an attempt to improve one's position is, in Hollywood, less a practice than a tradition), but it is indisputably one of the world's five most famous thoroughfares, and it did have a unique air—whereas Broadway was thought of as a theatrical district, Hollywood Boulevard was "such stuff as dreams are made on."

Near Hollywood's imaginary boundary with L.A., the Boulevard branched off Sunset Boulevard (there we go again) at Monogram Studio, Hollywood's easternmost film factory. From there it ran west-northwest for a few blocks, then, turning obliquely west at Vermont Avenue, it split the community in two as straight as the surveyors' line could make it. Eventually, somewhere west of Laurel Canyon, the site of dozens of love nests and their attendant love murders, it faded out in the West Hollywood Hills.

However, the Hollywood Boulevard known to tourists and visitors was much shorter than that; it was (and still is) a mile-long section in the middle of town, and from 1923 through 1926. I got to know it as well as the postman on the beat. For three years, barring weekends, holidays, and school vacations, I walked its length from Hollywood High School to Famous Players Lasky Studio five days each week. That key portion, already staking its claim to a place in legendry, started at the Gotham Deli, some two blocks west of the renowned Hollywood Hotel at Highland Avenue, ran past the Roosevelt Hotel with its intimate downstairs coffee shop, past Grauman's Chinese Theater, whose forecourt was beginning to register famous foot and palm prints for posterity in Caucasian cement, past the Montmartre Cafe, past Alec's Ice Cream and Malt Shop, past Grauman's Egyptian Theater and the Pickwick Book Store, past The Musso and Frank Grill and Henry's Restaurant, until it finally surrendered its significance at Hollywood and Vine. Beyond, there were a few tendrils: the Brown Derby, a half-block south on Vine Street and, a block further east, the American Legion Stadium, where every Friday night Hollywood's boxing aficionados came to watch the knockouts in and out of the ring.

The Hollywood Hotel, notorious for its midnight tocsin that sent wayward guests scurrying back to their own rooms, landed on the plus side when Carrie Jacobs Bond composed "A Perfect Day" on its parlor piano. Later, in the '30s, it made news for the last time before its demolition (no one expected anything in Hollywood to last, not even for historical interest) when it became the home base for a weekly radio hour of entertainment called, surprisingly, "Hollywood Hotel."

With Dick Powell as the M. C., the industry's musicians and entertainers filled most of the time slot, but the star turn was a gossip spot featuring Louella Parsons. Mrs. Parsons was an excellent reporter, better and less acidulous than most of her colleagues or successors, but that talent was completely overshadowed by a steady stream of malapropisms and by a nasal and amateurish delivery which has been mercilessly parodied to the present day.

At the end of the first program, Louella asked Powell if he had any recommendations. "Sure," said honest Dick. "Hire a good actress to read your stuff."

That was the last time Louella asked Dick's advice. From then on he couldn't make her column until they reconciled not long before his death.

For a nickel a tourist could hop a "Big Red Car" anywhere on the Boulevard and ride into the center of Los Angeles—if there were some unavoidable reason for making the trip. Outside the Monogram Studio the tourist would be delighted to get his first sight of movie-making—the good ship *Mayflower*, appearing as staunch as the day she had anchored off Plymouth Rock. It was all that remained of Charles Ray's lost gamble.

Ray's story is of interest because it is a story of failure, and failure; which is rarely tolerated in a movie plot, it is indigenous in the film world. If one in a thousand makes it as an actor, a writer, a director, or as a producer, it is not only a Big Break it is usually a Big Story. Only rarely will a Hollywood flack

Dick Powell, director Eddie Dmytryk and producer Adrian Scott. *Cornered*. RKO.

write a saga of a Hollywood flop, which, like the subtext of *A Star Is Born*, often carries more drama than any story of success.

They troop in by the thousands; they come by plane, by train, by car, by motorbike, or by thumb. Most are so young and starry-eyed they fail to see a ghostly sign at the city's entrance that says, "All hope abandon, ye who enter here." And, in a perverted way, that is the real tragedy of Hollywood: hope never dies and rarely alters its aim. Only a few will give up their dreams, accept reality, and try their luck on an easier mountain. The rest keep seeking Aladdin's lamp until they die. But even for those who find it, three wishes are often not enough.

Charles Ray Was Hollywood's original "clod-kicker," at least its first successful one. He made a fortune and a worldwide reputation playing bumpkins in films like Homer Comes Home *and* Alarm Clock Andy. *Then as the 'teens turned into the '20s he suffered a fatal attack of hubris, which was not unusual in his environment. He had escaped punishment for producing, directing, and playing the lead, but he went too far when he broke Hollywood's most respected taboo—he financed his own film. In 1922 he sank two million dollars into* The Courtship Of Miles Standish, *an unheard of amount at that time.*

The film was a total wipe-out.

For the rest of his fifty-two years he played bits, worked as an extra or, when he was lucky, as a "crowd assistant." Although, at thirty-one, he was not too old to start another life, he never left Hollywood. Here, at least, he had company. He was never on a set that didn't include a Maurice Costello, a Harry Meyers, or any of dozens of others who, when they reminisced about the other side of the rainbow, knew what they were talking about.

Whether they be small, like the Athens of Pericles, or relatively large, like the Italy of the Renaissance, an in-depth study of the attributes shared by "golden age" communities would be a worthy thesis in social science. Offhand it would seem that an uninhibited comradery, a closeness of minds regardless of class or status, an artistic (or scientific) humility, and the opportunity for frequent and open-handed exchange of tentative ideas are basic requirements. And the old Hollywood had them all. Power lunches were still far over the horizon, the Brahmin syndrome was the exclusive disease of Boston and India, and the concept that *any* man or woman might brilliantly erupt had never before been so totally accepted. In fact, the motto of the day was: "Be kind to the streetcar conductor; tomorrow he may be your producer." (Of course, that was a two-way street. I have seen producers become chauffeurs and executives become beggars.)

In my young eyes Henry's was the most interesting gathering place in town. Located on the north side of the Boulevard and a couple of doors west of Vine, it was the "easiest" restaurant I have ever known. Inside, its odd configuration featured two entry doors which flanked the cashier's counter. From there a patron walked down either side of a service and coffee bar which, along with its waiter, harbored a piano and a piano player. At the end of the bar a large, high-ceilinged room opened up to reveal a crowd of diners, some sitting, some table-hopping, and all animatedly sharing the latest developments with their friends.

The food was as good as any in town, but the real attraction was the clientele. In keeping with the studios' working hours the place was open all night. It was usually at its busiest when George Nichols Jr., another assistant, and I would wend our weary way there about 5:30 in the morning— dawn in pre-smog Hollywood was always a lovely sight. We would order "graveyard stew" all around (to those unfamiliar with haute cuisine, that's broken-up buttered toast in a bowl of steaming half-and-half) then sit back, breathe an end-of-the-workday sigh, and look around at our world: friends, colleagues, and occasional strangers who might one day be both. Saturday was special; Madam Francis dropped in for her weekly visit accompanied by a few of her newest girls—she believed it paid to advertise.

But the best show was often at the cashier's counter.

Like any exploding cultural center, Hollywood has had several heavy immigrations. Lured by the advent of sound, the migrants of the late 20s were not fleeing a mad dictator, as they would in the next decade; they were professionals—actors, singers, musicians, and dancers—who hoped to find in Hollywood a performers' paradise. Many of them, with the instincts of skilled mummers, knew where to go to make their presences known. It seemed that some hit Henry's before they checked into a hotel. No one declaimed "To be or not to be," but with the pianist's backing some sang, or, more often, danced.

Around the cashier's counter the brick floor was small but smooth, and it was there, away from the diners, that tap-dancers strutted their stuff. An occasional customer, entering or leaving, would stop for a moment to catch an intricate break or roll, and before moving on, smile his appreciation. And a smile is all it took to inspire an even greater effort, an effort which was always "give" and infrequently "get."

In the forecourt of the Chinese Theater visitors now stare at the hardened concrete prints of the Hollywood greats as though willing them to materialize before their eyes; on the Boulevard the stars of legends are sunk into the sidewalks of the "magic mile" throughout its length. Truly, they are the petrified spoor of dinosaurs who, in the golden years, walked this street in broad daylight, shopping at some of the better boutiques, browsing at the Pickwick Book Store, or just grabbing a taste of an environment they would soon leave behind.

Neither the Polaroid nor the paparazzi had yet been invented and a well-known star could parade the Boulevard openly, attracting only an occasional surprised stare, but never a personal onslaught. And a person with a sharp eye for "comers" could spot success in the making as a young Joan Crawford sashayed down the street with a friendly smile for everyone, or feel the chill of failure as an equally young James Murray reeled along the pavement carrying a brown-bagged bottle.

James Murray was just twenty-six when he lit up the Hollywood skies in King Vidor's The Crowd. Nine years later he hit bottom and died of drink. It is a curious fact that the use of drugs, especially alcohol, often increases in direct proportion to the amount of success achieved by Hollywood's creative core—its writers, directors, and especially actors. Drinking and doing drugs is more concurrent with an artist's success than with his failure, for success puts him on a pinnacle where he rarely feels comfortable. He has often heard "There is always room at the top," but his hyperactive imagination adds "because so many people keep falling off!"

While James Murray was still grappling with success John Carradine strolled the Avenue of the Stars trying to find it. Wearing a threadbare topcoat thrown loosely over his lanky frame *a la* John Barrymore, and his Barrymore hat cocked atop his scraggy head, he was more super than star, yet every inch a "strolling player." But the obvious were often overlooked.

The Cinegrill was a subterranean coffee shop in the Roosevelt Hotel which, by some miracle, had escaped the attention of thrill-seekers—even the native ones. A friend of mine was the resident pianist, and there I spent many a night over a cup of coffee. My friend played good one-finger jazz, but what really made the place jump musically were the Tin Pan Alley song writers then flooding Hollywood who frequented the cafe in the night's small hours. They were only too happy to spell the house musician, and their "and-then-I-wrote" renditions were mind-blowing reflections of another world.

Douglas Fairbanks and Charlie Chaplin often dropped in around midnight. They were followed closely by John Carradine, who would lower his spare body into the booth nearest the two stars. Some ten minutes later a bellhop would descend the stairs, announcing in a voice loud enough to cut through the music, "Call for John Carradine, a call for Mr. Carradine!" John would wait until the boy had made one circuit of the room, then raise a long, thin finger. "Here, boy!" He would flip the page a quarter (I always fantasized it was his last—and who knows?), walk slowly to the cashier, as though expecting a tap on his shoulder, pay for his coffee, and disappear up the stairs. The next night he would be back, and if Doug and Charlie were present there would be a repeat performance.

I never learned if Fairbanks or Chaplin ever used him in a film (much later, I did) but somehow Carradine made it. Once in a while a happy ending is a welcome thing even if it isn't a part of the original story.

I have slighted Musso-Frank's because that excellent tavern can speak for itself. It is still here, and going strong—the only golden age restaurant to survive the ghettoization of the Boulevard and its environs. Musso's menu is still the most varied in town and its patronage, though somewhat less film-folk oriented than in Hollywood's heyday, is stable enough to guarantee its continued existence.

For many years the Boulevard's most important crossroads were not in the center of town, but at the magic mile's eastern terminus. There it was given a human touch, not by a star, but by the best-known cop in the entire city.

Day after day he stood at the center of Hollywood and Vine, arms moving gracefully as he managed Hollywood's heaviest traffic with a skill rivaling that of Stokowski cajoling his orchestra. He was as firm as a good school teacher, as patient as a head waiter, and as demanding as the IRS, but the drivers loved him.

For a week or two before Christmas his post at the crossroads was engulfed daily by a huge pile of presents from friends, many of whom didn't know his name, and when progress finally tagged him as expendable "there wasn't a dry eye in the house." From then on, perhaps in subconscious revenge, more motorists ran the red than had ever disobeyed his outstretched palm.

And no one was moved to say "Merry Christmas" to the traffic signals that replaced him.

CHAPTER TWELVE

New York, New York…!

In 1930, film travel was a rare perk for a toiler of the second rank; even directors and producers usually stayed home, and by that time "home" for the great majority of film workers was Hollywood. But Paramount was still being taxed on their lot in Astoria, and it paid to keep it operational. Furthermore, many of Broadway's top artists were not yet eager to invade "iffy" territory. So, in keeping with the boast implied in its name, "Paramount Pictures" probably made more early talkies in New York than did any other major studio. Films as varied as Mamoulian's *Applause* and Lubitsch's *The Smiling Lieutenant* won critical kudos. But it took the Marx Brothers' *Animal Crackers* and *The Cocoanuts* to convince most of the hold-outs that sound had really added something new to the screen.

Although few viewers looked for content or significance in a Marx Brothers picture, they were there. The purely physical routines were in the tradition of the Comedia dell Arte and they would have been comfortably accommodated in a Mack Sennett production. There was the same sharp satire, disguised as slapstick, directed at High Society and figures of wealth and authority, but instead of deflating fat plutocrats or their minions, the cops, as Chaplin and his fellow comics had done, the Marx Brothers targeted that perfectly realized symbol of the upper classes, Margaret Dumont. Carrying the large build favored by the divas of the period, ostentatiously gowned and wearing floor-length ropes of pearls, she sailed through their films under full canvas, an insulated ark, oblivious to the Brothers' insults, slurs, and physical onslaughts.

Unfortunately, the wild humor of the textual scenes distracted most viewers from the deeper subtexts, whether they involved dilettantish art lovers in A Night At The Opera, *or the death-dealing makers of senseless wars, as in* Duck Soup. *However, if that had been all, the Marx Brothers would have been just another pebble in comedy's pond. Their distinction resided in something far beyond the capabilities of Sennett's silents, it rested on their manipulation of the contradictions inherent in the English language—or, their way with words. Although radio comedians like Fred and Steve Allen later used the technique skillfully, none equaled the impact of the zany quartet. Groucho (to Chico): "Call me a cab." Chico: "All right, you're a cab." This would hardly raise a titter today, but when first uttered, those simple words brought down the house. George Bernard Shaw spent half a lifetime and a fortune trying to eliminate the idiosyncrasies of English spelling, but it was the Marx Brothers, using the newly developed medium of the talkies, who first informed a guffawing English-speaking world that it had created a dangerously ambiguous vocabulary.*

(Many decades have flickered by since Hollywood was a discrete community, separated from Los Angeles and its other small suburbs by miles of orange orchards, acres of tomatoes and seasonally-grown poinsettias, fields of yellow mustard weed, sagebrush, and river beds which, though dry most of the year, flushed out the huge Los Angeles basin with flash floods during the rare two-inch killer storms. The neighborhood is now a ghetto, which the Hollywood Chamber of Commerce has long sought to renovate for the sake of tourists who come looking for glamour, and find stars in the pavement instead of in the flesh, and their footprints at the Chinese Theater. Within its imaginary boundaries there is only one major film studio. As used by the fans, the press, and gossip-mongers, the noun "Hollywood," no longer identifies a community but an industry (on very rare occasions, an art) whose aspects, activities, and articles of commerce were once called "the movies." In this sense, elements of Beverly Hills, Palm Springs, the Valley, Santa Barbara, and various other areas of greater Los Angeles are parts of that "Hollywood"—so is New York. This is my excuse for including it in a history of Hollywood.)

It was predictable that my first impression of Manhattan would relate to a film; a comparison to the "top-side" architecture of *Metropolis* was automatic. If one could view the city as a conglomeration of buildings devoid of mammalian life it would be unquestionably the first wonder of the modern world, and for an imperfect adult, arriving by train from what was essentially a transplanted mid-western environment, it was an unearthly sight. However, inhabitants are the personification of any town, and six months in Gotham shoved my sense of wonder well into the background.

Astoria's studio was faithful to its locale: a single wall-bound structure in which the stages were arranged vertically rather than horizontally, with offices, cutting and projection rooms stuffed into whatever space was available. Compared to Hollywood's plants it was a bit of a joke, but plants don't make pictures, and a couple of excellent sound films had already been made there. More were to come. Those films, and the occasional glimpses of a nude Harpo chasing some half-frightened secretary or extra through the building's spooky corridors, lent the decrepit structure a skewed sort of sophistication, which was diminished by the presence of the entrenched, somewhat loutish "bully-boy" operators in the projection booths.

By June of 1930 the Great Depression was a blight on the land, and in New York the suffering of the people was more evident than it had been in Hollywood. Here some men and women toted trays of apples which they sold for five cents each; men dressed in tailored business suits begged in the streets, offering embossed calling cards as guarantees that they would repay a loan of a dollar or two if given the lender's address; hotdog cart restaurateurs fought for favorable corners; a cab driver would bare his head in thanks for a quarter tip; and a very good six-course dinner could be had for a dollar. There was as yet no unemployment insurance and a man, woman, or child could starve to death in the streets. (The more things change, etc.)

Perhaps the only good thing that could be said about the Great Depression was that it was impartial—it was hell for the jobless of all classes. But it was not too bad for the lucky worker and his family. Unlike the recession of 1988-93, food prices went down, not up, and if he had to forgo a Christmas bonus or take a cut in salary, the drop in the cost of living enabled him to sustain life at a decent level. That is, if he could dismiss the fear of "fear itself."

For a youth of twenty-one the state of the union was not a deep concern. An expense account of seventy-five dollars, which matched my normal salary, gave me a total of 150 dollars a week and put me in the top five percent of the time. My room at the still uncompleted Barbizon Plaza Hotel cost eighteen dollars a week, and the subway was a nickel a ride. Except for the busy hours of the day I was living in clover.

When so-called grid-lock on an L.A. freeway gets me down, I recall Manhattan's crosstown traffic and count my blessings. At the end of my first full working day on the lot I shared a cab with George Cukor back to my hotel, or so I hoped. The few blocks from the studio to the Queens Bridge on-ramp was no sweat, but the crush on the bridge and across the island was molasses in January, even in July. I jumped out of the cab, asked Cukor to pick me up when he caught up with me, and started to walk. When I reached my hotel, halfway across Manhattan, Cukor and the cab were not yet in sight. From then on I walked home every day unless I could miss the busy hours by quitting early or working late.

New York wasn't all bad. The zoos, museums, and art galleries were tops; the restaurants, especially when variety of cuisine was considered, were matchless; and Broadway had the American monopoly on first-run theater, which was generally considered a plus. But for someone brainwashed by the movies it was a disappointment. Although I had seen and heard what filmmakers called "theatrical" acting in the work of recruits in the early talkies, the pretensions and affectations of much of the legitimate theater were impossible to accept. Especially unbelievable were the juveniles and ingénues fresh out of dramatic schools, but on occasion a seasoned artist could move me to forget his devices and to identify with his character.

For me, and for millions of people throughout the world, the two-dimensional shadows on the screen were more spontaneous and seductive than the flesh and blood elocutionists of the living stage. Strange as it may seem, polls show that most viewers find it easier to empathize with the photographed images than with the live actors whose very corporeality keeps them at bay, and whose every gesture and word has been planned and practiced for weeks or months. Unfortunately, except for a few true artists, the mechanics of their trade show through.

Actors who come to Hollywood from the theater invariably assure their friends they will often revisit their artistic roots to "recharge their batteries." Few do. Many years ago Katherine Hepburn convinced Spencer Tracy that he could rejuvenate his skills on Broadway—or so he told me. The play was a success, but to the surprise and chagrin of the cast, who had anticipated a long, long run, after a few weeks Tracy dropped out of the show.

"I just couldn't take it," he said. "The same words, the same reactions, the same people, night after night after night! The same words...!"

And in the theater, according to George M. Cohan, Spencer Tracy was the best.

Cornered, 1945.

There have been better regional orchestras than the New York Philharmonic and better dance companies than the New York City Ballet, but in
one form of entertainment the Big Apple reigned supreme—vaudeville.
Ah, the Palace—*that* was an institution! On those rare occasions when
some startling potential development—like a colony on the moon or a possible cure is for a failing memory—makes me feel that I was born too soon,
I think of the Palace Theater and realize how lucky I was to have made the
cut. For in 1932 the Palace became history. There had been, of course,
nationwide chains of vaudeville houses which circulated a wide variety of
entertainers throughout the United States and Canada, but the Palace presented the cream of the crop. whether they were acrobats, jugglers, slack-
wire artists, impressionists, actors (usually in comedy skits), magicians, dancers, singers, comedians, or rope-twirlers, each was the best in his line. It was

another world, a dedicated class apart, whose members shared two qualities in common: a matchless talent for establishing a complete rapport with the audience and a superlative gift for entertaining.

Some years later, when I started working with actors, I found that vaudevillians, burlesque comedians, and night club entertainers generally made the smoothest transition to screen acting, probably because establishing a personal one-on-one involvement with the members of the audience was second nature. Such a relationship may seem illogical given the vast separation in place and time between the screen actor and his viewers; nevertheless, millions of filmgoers will attest to its existence. I have found it easy to walk out on a play, a film, or a ballet, but I never walked out of the Palace until the curtain dropped on the closing act. It would have been as unthinkable as walking out on a friend in the middle of his favorite anecdote.

I often wished I could walk out of Astoria, where recording and editing facilities were deplorably outdated. New York had surrendered its claim to serious production years before sound, but the remnants still in operation seemed to care little about the state of the art. Three years after *The Jazz Singer* the studio still used the outmoded Movietone technique, printing picture and track side by side on a single strip of 35mm film—but not exactly side by side.

For projecting purposes sound had to be printed some nineteen frames ahead of its matching picture, and that made cutting a matter of guesswork on the part of the editor and demanded blind trust on the part of the director and/or producer.[30] They could not see a properly finished cut until the first answer print (the first complete print made from the cut negative) was available. And once the negative had been cut, re-editing was an extremely difficult operation which, in effect, left the film editor largely responsible for the film's final look.

Perhaps our directors had not the requisite clout to bring the studio up to snuff, but before our film was finished Ernst Lubitsch came to town. He was scheduled to shoot *The Smiling Lieutenant* with Chevalier, Colbert, and Miriam Hopkins at Astoria, and Lubitsch was always in charge. He insisted on separate sound for his dailies, even in the face of a threatened strike. The twenty seconds needed to thread up the extra sound reel had upset the projectionists' lackadaisical routine, but it was hardly worth a walkout, and Lubitsch got his way. However, such differences between the attitudes of the East Coast and West Coast unions hampered working relationships for many years, and made a rare location trip to New York an unsavory experience. It was easier on the nerves and the pocketbook to build a brownstone street on the back lot.

One of the more friendly spots in New York was the studio commissary. There I often had a coffee with our film director, Cyril Gardner, while giving him a rundown on the current dailies. Cyril had been a child actor, then a film editor, and had acquired a small reputation as a man of quirks, one of which was his refusal to drink coffee from the commissary's thick mugs—so he brought in his own delicate china.

During one of these mid-morning coffee breaks I spotted a natty gentleman walking toward the studio's main entrance. He wore a gray vest, gray spats, striped trousers, a cutaway coat, and a derby hat. He also carried a cane. I assumed he was an actor reporting for a late call, but Gardner suggested I wait a few minutes. A short time later the same man walked through the kitchen door of the commissary. Now dressed in the tieless shirt and white apron of the usually-unnoticed busboy, he went quietly about his business of clearing the tables. I thought it was an odd way to attract attention, since neither a morning suit nor a busboy's uniform was an unusual sight in a movie studio, but Gardner mentioned that a man named Pasternak had used the same means at the same studio toward the same end some years before, and he had been noticed. Joe was now producing successful musicals in Berlin.

"If it works," said Cyril, "don't knock it." And I stopped smirking.[31]

I had arrived in New York in June—on New Year's Eve I sneaked out of town in a state matching that of the economy. A serious case of flu had me fighting DTs all the way to Chicago. When I arrived in Pasadena, Hollywood's preferred detraining point in the L.A. area, I quickly recovered. While blinking the last of the New York cinders out of my eyes, I looked up at the sweet-smelling azure sky, then knelt and kissed the boards of the station platform. Although for me there was no real place called home, this was close. It was warm, the landscape wore every color but white, and no one was selling apples. What's more, we had Herbert Hoover's solemn word that we were turning the corner and we could soon count on "a car in every garage and a chicken in every pot."

Chapter Thirteen

Good art never mirrors nature—even a good photograph is a consciously manipulated angle—but it is often said, either in praise or in defense, that art mirrors society. Whether this is good for society is a matter of opinion, and Hollywood, which is often confused in times of change, could not decide what its distorted looking-glass should reflect—was society symbolized by the ruined millionaire jumping out of a thirty-story window or by the mobster getting rich peddling bootleg gin? Or was it the breadlines? After all, though times were hard they had not yet been dubbed "the Great Depression," and many assumed that, like a plague, it was only a question of time before it died of its own evils. Even the most cynical of pessimists would not have guessed that it would last a decade, to be eliminated at last only by a prolonged war that would make our nation prosperous while leaving others in ruins.

At twenty-two, I was neither cynical nor pessimistic, but I got a sudden dose of reality in that first week of January, 1931, when I reported back to Paramount. I found I had no job. It was the start of a personal depression that lasted for seven months—and this is where, as many old-timers will understand, the Schwabs came into the picture. Earlier I mentioned that Joe Oblath carried many a chit, but in a community like Hollywood that situation is not newsworthy; in a field as capricious and unreliable as filmmaking where hundreds, even thousands, of self-defined "talents," crowd the streets, carrying a number of out-at-the-elbows hopefuls was not an unusual undertaking. More than a few of Hollywood's shops, markets, and restaurants occasionally helped out a strapped customer.

But the Schwab brothers, who owned and ran a drug store where Laurel Canyon debouches onto Sunset Boulevard, were big time when it came to charity; they were the most tolerant and the most forgiving Fairy Godfathers in Hollywood. One might say they had an instinct for recognizing a human being who was near the end of his rope, and the humanity to do something about it. And certainly, in my experience, they never dunned a defaulting debtor. If some eager immigrant wised up or decided he had had enough, packed up and, without settling his debts, headed for home, Schwab's simply closed the account. Or if, as occasionally happened, someone suddenly hit the jackpot and, blinded by the bright lights of success, forgot his benefactors, their reaction was the same. As a result they were one of the most highly regarded trios in show business.

Schwab's became a meeting place for Hollywood names and for those who were hoping make the club. An aspirant could never be sure, only hope, that a chance meeting might lead to the big break. That feeling was so strong that a seat at Schwab's lunch and soda counter has gone down in Hollywood's anecdotal history as the stool Lana Turner occupied when she was discovered by the owner of the Hollywood Reporter, *although the actual site of that miracle was more than a mile down the Boulevard.*

Sometime in the '30s, Sid Skolsky, a syndicated Hollywood columnist, made Schwab's his home away from home, giving it more publicity than it really needed, and it has never been decided whether Skolsky made Schwab's or Schwab's made Skolsky. As one who profited from the Schwabs' kindness to the needy, I prefer to think the latter.

After seven months of waning hope I finally rejoined the Paramount cutting department, but this time as a first cutter, and I finally learned why I had been so summarily dismissed. It was not that the studio's editorial department was being pared down, but that it was being built up to save some films. During my six-month stint in New York a new executive, George M. Arthur, had replaced the previous head of the department and in obedience to the old adage "A new broom sweeps clean" the studio's old cutters were being dropped to make way for the new.

Sometime in the mid-'20s Warners had absorbed First National Studios and in the process had inherited the best group of film editors in Hollywood. Over the next few years, driven probably by a distaste for the sloppy cutting imposed by the shortcomings of Vitaphone, these superior craftsmen left Warners one by one. And one by one George Arthur picked them up to work for Paramount. It was clearly not a question of nepotism or old-boy favoritism but the upgrading of talent, so those who stood in their way went quietly.

The incoming editors were by reputation the best in the business. And though there were a few other first-rate editors here and there, no other studio could claim such an outstanding cluster of cutters who, over the next ten years, had a strong hand in establishing Paramount pictures as not necessarily the best but certainly the most polished, well-structured and, as the critics put it, the "slickest" films in town.

Admired by the technique-oriented and belittled by the "kitchen sink" school of art lovers, those qualities were not the result of editing alone. The slickest cutting in the world can't overcome weak writing, inadequate directing, or misguided acting, but just as a savory sauce can make boiled cauliflower a culinary delight, so good editing can make deficient flicks less unpalatable.

Before script form was standardized, some writers followed theatrical conventions and arranged their material into scenes and acts. Others developed their stories sequentially to take advantage of the medium's opportunities for the almost limitless use of sets and locations.[32] However, in careless hands, sequence structure sometimes took the plot into seductive but deceptive byways which, if they escaped the director's attention (and they often did) resulted in the filming of scenes whose irrelevance was not obvious until the film was viewed as an edited whole.

(It may be hard to believe but there were directors who found it impossible to refrain from filming every wayward whim. And for those who, like von Stroheim, insisted on following where fancy led, freedom could be a mortal danger.)

As Hollywood gained more confidence and a bigger audience its films became more elaborate and filming costs increased. Producers sought to save money by anticipating ill-conceived material before going on the floor. On looking over production personnel their eyes fell on their gifted editors, whose craftsmanship, at its best, had always carried a touch of magic, and whose intuitive ability to spot an incompatible sequence or set-up was unmatched. On the assumption that such talent should not be immured in the cutting room but put to work before a crime was committed, Arthur and the management agreed to give the editor a slot on the set. It was understood that he would always be available to offer suggestions or advice concerning the film's editing needs, but only if they were requested. A close relationship between editor and director was nothing new, but the establishment of such a practice as a standard policy was unique.

Since editors were now on the set, the first cuts were made under their supervision by glorified assistants called first cutters—naturally. In post-production most editors took over the hands-on editing to completion, while others trusted their first cutters to finish the job. The system had many advantages, among them (1) the invaluable set experience that helped a number of editors become directors, (2) the opportunity afforded the first cutters to hone their skills (which are never learned by just looking on), and (3) occasionally, it was welcomed by a director.

The best directors rarely felt the need for advice while the worst were too insecure to ask for it; consequently, the philosophically-inclined editor spent much of his set time studying character (a necessary constituent of the director's craft) not with his subjects on a couch but under working conditions. As mentioned earlier, a studio was a total community, and the set incorporated as provocative a group of guinea pigs as one could hope to find. Identities, personalities, temperaments, facades, strengths, and frailties inevitably surfaced, especially when the shooting schedule was long enough for the mix to shake down and open up.[33] Aside from the occasional actor, the director was usually the most labyrinthine person on the set, in large part because he enjoyed a disarticulated job[34], faced the greatest array of out-of-the-blue problems, and was saddled with an inescapable obligation to make an endless number of decisions daily. His manner of dealing with this sea of troubles displayed his character at its best or at its worst.

At Paramount the director's problems might suffer an overload from the first hour of the first day on the set, evoking a reaction that could escape no one's attention. The mere presence of a possible "advisor" on the set was anathema to a director who fancied himself an auteur, no matter what the reality. However, there were degrees. Although it is true that no filmmaker has complete confidence in his work, the really good director demonstrated at least a working amount of self-assurance by welcoming a bouncing board, another mind against which to test tentative ideas, or give-and-take sessions that might lead to a broader understanding of a concept under consideration. When nagging questions challenged solutions he knew a two-sided examination could be a help, if only to reveal a problem not previously noticed; at worst, it could do him no harm.

On the other hand, the less talented (and more frequently encountered), directors refrained asking for help, and usually avoided speaking to the editor lest other members of the crew should consider it a sign of insecurity. The shakiest among them showed symptoms of paranoia if the editor even talked with another member of the company, assuming that he and his shortcomings must be the subject of any off-to-the-side conversations.

Nevertheless the practice was continued at Paramount through the '30s, '40s, and into the '50s, and the studio continued to have the slickest films in the world.

In the early '30s, society's mirror reflected two major scenes: breadlines and "the mob." Breadlines, which vividly dramatized the poverty of the millions of unemployed, were too downbeat for entertainment but—the mob! Now there were men who were making it in spite of the Depression, and making it big. Since the eighteenth Amendment had guaranteed that only those outside the law could gratify the nation's thirst, who better to inspire a cynical society? So, led by Warner Brothers, several studios decided to glorify the gangster, but surreptitiously. No studio could admit to ennobling anyone or anything illicit, and they posed as patriots exposing the evils of society, especially the evils born of prohibition. However, no one was too surprised when it was found that playing evil characters was the fast elevator to success, an elevator ridden by Paul Muni, James Cagney, Edward G. Robinson, Humphrey Bogart, and assorted others. And hardly anyone saw an inconsistency.

The appeal of these admired villains mirrored the appeal of the villain-heroes of an earlier time: the James Boys, the Dalton Gang, Butch Cassidy and the Sundance Kid, and those other Kids named Cisco and Billy. After all, how different in spirit was the St. Valentine's Day massacre in Chicago from the shootout at the O. K. Corral in Tombstone? Whether gangsters or gunmen, the chief participants were a law unto themselves, and exactly the kind of heroes every man and boy suffering from restrictive parents, an exacting employer, a treadmill job, or a nagging wife, could admire and aspire to be. They "wore no man's collar," and it mattered little if they killed other gangsters (good riddance) or greedy bankers (good riddance). And although these evildoers were obliged to die to satisfy the code, only bad gangsters died whimpering; the good gangsters always died like men.

A few years later, when the Volstead Act was repealed and the mob was no longer performing a public service, roles were sometimes switched.

More often now the hero was a G-man, say, Elliot Ness, but he still blew away his share of victims without reading them their rights while skirting the law he had sworn to uphold.

(Their appeal will never die; thirty-five years later Bonnie and Clyde were the bad guys to be admired, not the nameless spoilsports who cut short their exhilarating careers. And as a comment on how our tastes improve with time, in 1992, the New York critics named *Goodfellas*, the most sadistically brutal mob movie to date, the best film of the year.)

Paramount ignored the turmoil of the Depression and the social revolution which resulted. It hewed to its tried and true with only von Sternberg and George Raft as their nod to the trend. Schulberg's preference for heavy drama was more than counterbalanced by Ernst Lubitsch's talent for high comedy which, though sophisticated, was still not too subtle for the average viewer.

Lubitsch was near the top of Hollywood's long list of anomalies, a list which includes Chaplin, Garbo, and Cary Grant. They made or starred in some of the most prestigious films in motion-picture history, and none of them won an Oscar. Lubitsch came to stay in 1922, and although he was Berlin-born and had learned his trade while making a slew of German pictures, his acclimatization to the American scene and its society, with its dreams, its tastes, and its foibles, was little short of miraculous. For the next thirty years he was Hollywood's most consistent and successful filmmaker. And although it is as rare as a clear conscience, the "Lubitsch touch" remains the most desired goal of every director working in his genre. His only outright box office failure was *Broken Lullaby*, a somber anti-war film made in 1931, but even on that he left his mark—so to speak.

It may not have been the first film to undergo a title change, but it was probably the first to suffer it as an attempt at resuscitation. Under its original title, The Man I Killed, *it was a financial disaster, and under its cozy new title,* Broken Lullaby, *it was a financial disaster. It isn't that easy to fool the viewers.*

Technically it was a standout for its time, and also a perfect example of a studio maxim: technique can help but it won't make a picture. One shot in the film was especially startling—and counterproductive. To my knowledge it was the first time a camera dollied around an actor in a full, 360-degree circle. Filmwise people knew that to make the shot all lights had to be placed overhead to be out of camera range, and it was considered a technical tri-

Humphrey Bogart and Jean Porter in *The Left Hand of God*. 1955, Twentieth Century Fox.

umph. Unfortunately, it broke another of filmmaking's few basic rules—it was also seen as a technical gem by the viewers, most of whom spent the duration of the shot marveling at the director's ingenuity rather than absorbing the substance of the scene—which, in any case, was a triumph for the man who did the lighting, not the director.

The 360-degree set-up has since become a show-off shot, a staple used by cinema students and new directors seeking to impress their colleagues in the audience, but it is "more honored in the breach than the observance." When the fledgling abandons the shot for good, he's getting somewhere.

After Schulberg's departure in 1932, Paramount followed Lubitsch's lead and concentrated on comedy. Using to advantage the talents of writers like Claude Binyon and the Brackett-Wilder team along with stars like Kay Francis, Claudette Colbert, Charles Ruggles, Mary Boland, Charles Laughton, and Carole Lombard, it turned out some of the most successful and far-out comedies of the decade, while the Marx Brothers, W. C. Fields, and Mae West left their indelible prints on the history of the Golden Years.

Mae West was one of a kind, a rarity, a phenomenon who made the most of a narrow talent to become one of the outstanding entertainers of her time. Although anything but a sex goddess or a perfect ten, she made sex a best-selling commodity. And because she knew that the delivery is often less interesting than the promise, she never made the mistake, so common today, of pandering to the voyeurs. She was aware of her shortcomings and was smart enough to turn them into advantages.

She was very short, and her extremely high heels, usually hidden by period gowns, imparted a suggestive sway to her sauntering walk—she always took her time. With a little help from corsets and supportive gowns, she transformed a dumpy figure into a modern version of the hourglass shape of the Gay Nineties.

Her face was a mask bearing a slight, scornful smile which portrayed her attitude toward her world and the men she suffered to occupy it. With a light snort, she delivered her lines in a brassy monotone, so she knew they had to be wisecracks; no matter how close she came to crossing the censor's line, she did it with humor. She fully realized that a Mae West character who took sex seriously would be unbelievable.

But she was all warmth and laughter when with the broken-down ex-pugilists she loved and with whom she surrounded herself (her father had been a fighter). She supported many of them privately, and by furnishing them with long runs in her films. And there probably wasn't one who would have hesitated to sacrifice his life for her if the occasion demanded it.

Mae West worked hard at maintaining her image, even between takes or films. One of her frequent routines was the next morning telephone call, which she always took on the set phone when surrounded by grips and electricians. In a loud and clear voice she would conduct a postmortem on her activities of the previous evening, which, of course, were sexually oriented. Yet she never uttered an off-color word. Although a bit embarrassed at first, the crew members soon caught on to the act. They realized she was looking for the reactions she enjoyed while probably trying out dialogue for her next script. She wrote much of her own material.

Like most artists she was protective of her work. When we sneak-previewed The Belle of the Nineties *(which McCarey directed and I cut), a line delivered by the leading man brought down the house. At next morning's editorial conference I was instructed to find a smooth way to delete the line, even though she had written it. Leo just smiled and turned to Miss West when I protested that the laugh was good for the picture and therefore good for her. The discussion was cut very short, and I cut the line out of the film.*

One other incident is worth mentioning: one of Miss West's songs was backed up by a wonderful choir of black singers dressed as "darkies" beatin' their feet on the docks of New Orleans. This was 1932, and no matter how hard she tried, she was not allowed to sing in the immediate presence of the chorus. Instead, she sang at her bedroom window while her back-up, apparently half a mile away, sang with her yet not with her. Whenever I feel defeated by the slow progress in the field of human relations, I remember cutting this scene and I realize that we are making headway, however slowly.

And one more item that will never find a place in the history books: Mae West was the best lip-syncher I have ever known.

Chapter Fourteen

"Every action has an equal and opposite reaction."

So, roughly, wrote Isaac Newton some 350 years ago. Today one can only wonder if that most brilliant of men realized that his third law of motion applied equally to the world outside of science, and that wherever morals, ethics, and values were taken seriously, that law of dynamics also prevailed. Still, Galileo's treatment at the hands of the Catholic Inquisition must have warned Newton that whenever an advance in knowledge and the means to disseminate it impart a forward movement in standards and values, the opposite reaction, in the form of censorship, is always part of the package. For instance:

(1) "Shurlock [the censor] says four shots are too many for Pony [a cowboy] to fire into the barber. He considers this number of shots excessively brutal and gruesome. This depends primarily on how you shoot the shooting…[perhaps] in such a way that we can get out after two shots. The British and foreign censors are cracking down even more than the Code on this sort of thing."

(2) "Shurlock, the British censor, and some other censors now eliminate, without exception, any kicking in a fight, whether or not it is out of the frame."

(3) "I agree that it would not be good to include any shot of Gannon's hand with the knife in it. Even so, we should avoid…sadism or undue gruesomeness."

These are only three of the many recommendations—demands, really—made by the censor, Geoffry Shurlock, and transmitted to me in an interoffice memo by Frank McCarthy, 20th Century Fox's liaison with the Breen office, on October 9, 1958. It related to potentially censorable areas in the script of *Warlock*, a Western we were about to make. The leading players were Henry Fonda, Richard Widmark, and Anthony Quinn. This, too, is chronologically out of sequence, but it will serve as an example of the Code as it existed for over three decades. During that time its application remained essentially unchanged. (To satisfy the curious, the disposition of these recommendations will be addressed later in this chapter.)

My first contact with the fruits of censorship came in the mid-'20s when I was still a projectionist and scarcely knew the meaning of the word. In what turned out to be more a quiet stag party than a conference on unacceptable film concepts, the studio executives crowded into one of our small viewing rooms to "analyze" a few reels of film containing scenes that had been excised from Hollywood's product in response to non-resistible complaints from censor groups.

There was some nudity in extreme long shots from the Italian version of *Dante's Inferno*, but most of the culled material would hardly disturb a huddle of pre-schoolers today. Perhaps the steamiest scene in the collection showed a "wild party" in which an inebriated guest unraveled a sweater worn by Clara Bow, in due time exposing her chemise!

There have been numerous reasons advanced for the establishment of Hollywood's self-imposed Code, and for its abject surrender to the blue-nose fringe of our society. The truth is that the studios fought harder to protect their First Amendment rights than to curb film's growing licentiousness. In the end they surrendered, but only when their pocketbooks were at risk.

They were hit fore and aft by both the old countries and the new. With the exception of Ireland, where a constrictive Catholicism ruled the roost, European religious reaction was moderate—after all, it had exported its rabid puritans to the Americas over the last several centuries. But Europe's political restraints were, on the whole, more rigid than the West's, and its censors were primarily concerned with politics and internal government problems. On the other hand, in the United States and Canada religious fundamentalism was the chief enemy of the media's freedom of expression.

Flushed with their post-World War I victory over "John Barleycorn," every community, no matter how small, and every organization for the reform of this or that, appointed its own watchdog to sniff out sin in Hollywood's films. Religious groups organized committees to monitor the morals of their children and their neighbors, temperance societies objected to Hollywood's depiction of the widespread drinking Volstead had failed to stop, and civic organizations, especially metropolitan police departments, objected violently (and actively) to any implication of graft or corruption. Nothing was immune to attack from some group and often, after feeling the cutting edge of a local censor's shears, little that was recognizable as a 'story' was returned to the distributor. But that was not the worst of it.

Each of the groups now had the means to blackmail the filmmakers, and no matter how noble their pitch, they were more than willing to trade their ideals for a comfortable payoff. Something had to be done.

In 1922, Hollywood's scrapping entrepreneurs had surprised the film world by forming a loose Balkanized, confederation. The chief, perhaps the only, purpose of the Motion Picture Producers and Distributors of America (MPPDA) was to defend the studios and their distributing outlets against scattershot censorship. Deciding to fight fire with fire, they hired a Presbyterian elder of unblemished character to be the organization's "Czar." Besides a strong church background, Will Hays had an added advantage: he was a potent political VIP in the Harding administration. Taking his duties seriously, Hays decided that an inoculation of watered-down self-censorship might serve to disarm the mid-Victorian monitors of morality. He overestimated the good faith of the studios and underestimated the vigilance of society's self-appointed guardians.

In a partnership as loose and ineffective as the Yugoslav Federation there were, as yet, no specific taboos, only broad guidelines which allowed each studio head a good deal of latitude. Producers and directors established their own standards of decent behavior which, like the filmmakers, varied from the ideal to the idiotic.

One of the more whimsical results of the guidelines was an upgrading of the ages-old "buddy" system. Some producers now insisted that the leading man be strong, straight, and serious, a type to whom the possession of humor was denied.[35] However, with only a few exceptions, filmmakers realized that a film without laughs can be monotonous and, in entertainment, monotony breeds audience apathy; a whiff of laughing gas is a part of a good scenario's recipe even if, as is often the case in unbearable suspense, it is gallows humor.

To furnish the required levity while respecting the hero's dignity, the "buddy" became a fixture. A comedian like Jack Oakie was usually the leading man's Charlie McCarthy, while in Westerns, a character like Walter Brennan, riding at the side of his straight man, John Wayne, got all the funny lines and often the supporting-actor Oscar. The buddy could also be plot-useful; Roy Rogers' sidekick, "Gabby" Hayes, could be stupid enough to ask the obvious question which elicited the expository answer. He could ogle the pretty girl in the passing parade and even, on occasion, be vulgar and crude—as long as he got his laughs his peccadilloes were forgiven.

Leading ladies also suffered, or benefited from, the presence of "best friends" or "faithful servants." When a situation in Gone With The Wind *became unbearable for Scarlett or Melanie it was Hattie McDaniel who got the laughs which eased the tension, at least for the spellbound viewers.*

But once more the old-school graduates, directors like Capra, McCarey, and Stevens, in cooperation with multitalented actors such as Jimmy Stewart, Cary Grant, and Gary Cooper saved the day by restoring humor to the stars where it had always belonged.

After a decade of hit-and-miss cooperation and increasing public pressure, Hays realized that self-censorship was akin to anarchy. In 1932, the MPPA adopted a Production Code in which restraints on sex, socially unacceptable language, and extreme violence were written on "tablets of stone." And, since incorrigibles can be deterred only by suitable punishment, no film could be released without a Production Seal of Approval to verify that they had "sinned no more." Few producers felt that an off-color joke or a gruesome tidbit justified a drop in box office take and from then on, for thirty-four years, censorship was a prime concern for every film.

Iconoclasm is always dangerous, especially in Hollywood, where gossip is considered more real than fact, and principles are often concealed lest they be ridiculed, but the truth is that few directors were bothered by the Code. I never heard McCarey, or Cukor, or Taurog, or any director of quality bewail the censor's fiats. However, the system was not faultless and one of its problems was that the censor, in his preliminary review, rarely talked with the man who was to make the film; he based his recommendations on what he found in the script, and the difference between the script and the director's concept could be minute or monumental. It should be no surprise that the seasoned director knew the Code as well as anyone, and long before the script was sent to the censor the filmmaker had probably started the process of creating other, non-censorable ways to rewrite, stage, or eventually manipulate the editing of the questionable scenes. As to feeling restricted, that's hogwash.

Eddie teaching, 1979-80.

Any director who couldn't solve a simple problem of acceptability in a positive way could hardly be called a creative artist.

When speaking of censorship we're speaking of much more than freedom of speech or thought. The Ten Commandments are full of "thou shalt nots," yet no one, however irreligious, would publicly recommend their banishment. We have hundreds of thousands of laws that censor some action or other, be it murder, incest, or calumny. As for freedom of speech, the injunction against crying "Fire!" in a crowded hall or theater is well-known to all. Even a purely vocal disturbance of the peace is punishable by fine or imprisonment.

We were shooting a sequence for The End Of The Affair *at that shrine to permissive oratory, the Speakers Corner in Hyde Park. The English are uncom-*

monly well-mannered while watching a movie company's strange activities, but that morning an impish little Irish woman, still dressed in pajamas and bathrobe, was enjoying our show. Two or three times she disappeared for a few minutes, and at each reappearance she was more unstable in movement and more stentorian in voice. Finally she felt moved to sing her repertoire of pub songs, which appeared to be extensive. We begged her to stop while we were shooting—to no avail. The attendant police tried to shut her up—to no avail. In the end, accompanied by the cheers of the admiring crowd, the bobbies hauled her off in the paddy wagon as a public nuisance. And all this happened in the cradle of free speech.

"License" is defined as "freedom of action, speech, or thought, permitted or conceded," but it is also defined as "disregard of legal or moral restraints." The 'license' of the first definition would be accepted by a great majority of Americans, but as a standard of behavior, its extension would muster only minimal support. And it is the license of the second mode, under the euphemism of "freedom of expression," that so many filmmakers choose to support and protect.

If excessive violence, profanity, and vulgarity were used only when dramatically necessary there would be little valid objection, but that isn't so. Filmmakers, to a painful degree, now pander to voyeurs, masochists, sadists, and the emotionally skewed who need sexual titillation.

Perhaps the sensible argument is that one can think of no great film of the Golden Years that was made less effective by the exclusion of profanity, violence for the sake of violence, or unbridled and vulgar sex. Nor can one name a modern film which has been improved by their inclusion.[36]

Which leads us to the expedients taken to accommodate the censor's demands on *Warlock*.

(The scenes immediately preceding the first of Shurlock's objections were as follows: The members of Abe's gang are leaving the town of Warlock after a bawdy evening. But Pony is getting a late-night shave from a very frightened town barber. As Pony's friends shout out their departure, Pony makes a sudden move in the chair and is nicked by the barber's razor. In a rage, he hauls the barber out onto the raised boardwalk.)

(1) Shurlock considered four shots into the Barber's body too many, especially for the foreign censors. We decided to go them one better—we not only cut down the number of shots, but showed their effect in a unique way. (What little dialogue there was in the sequence is deleted.)

MEDIUM FULL SHOT   EXT. BARBER SHOP   NIGHT
Pony throws the barber off the boardwalk and out of the shot.

MEDIUM CLOSE SHOT   BARBER   EXT. STREET NIGHT
He stumbles into the shot and collides with the butt end of the barrel-shaped water wagon. Scared stiff, he turns to face Pony, backing into the water wagon.

MED. FULL SHOT   PONY
He jumps off the boardwalk and mounts his horse.

MED. CLOSE SHOT   BARBER
Frozen in fear, he stares at Pony (o. s.).

MED. FULL SHOT   PONY
Turning toward the barber he pulls his gun and fires twice.

CLOSE SHOT   BARBER
The bottom frame cuts him just below the neck. The jerk of his head indicates that he has been hit below the frameline. He reacts in surprise then, still staring at Pony (o. s.) he slowly slides down out of shot. The camera pans down with him but stops as his sagging body discloses two bullet holes in the water-wagon, both spouting water like low-powered fountains.

MED. FULL SHOT   SIDE ANGLE
*   ACROSS BUTT OF WATER-WAGON*
Gannon [Richard Widmark] and his brother, Billy [Frank Gorshin] ride by, glance momentarily at the spouting water in the foreground of shot, then ride on.

There was no blood, no wound, no objection from the censor, only an effective montage of a senseless killing.

(2) Shurlock referred to elimination of kicking in the fight. Rarely did competent directors resort to kicking, which is unimaginative and cliché. There are exceptions, but this was not one of them. (This refers to the next scene.)
(3) Shurlock wrote it would not be good to include any shot of Gannon's

hand with a knife in it. (Note: the sentence was ambiguous; he meant with a knife through *it.)*

In this sequence Gannon rides alone to the ranch house occupied by Abe's gang. At the start of the film Gannon had been a member of Abe's outfit, but now he is a deputy sheriff and he comes to warn Abe not to come to town in anger. His confrontation with Abe (Tom Drake) leads to a fight and, outnumbered, Gannon draws his gun.

FULL SHOT   GANNON, ABE, AND GANG   INT. HOUSE
                                                                            NIGHT
> *Gannon butts Abe back out of shot, then draws his gun, which is promptly knocked out of his hand by one of Abe's henchmen. It drops to the floor and slides under a wooden table. Gannon moves forward to retrieve it but is tripped and falls to the floor.*

MED. SHOT   GANNON ON FLOOR
> *He scrambles for his gun, retrieves it and, putting his free hand on the table top for support, he starts to get up.*

MED. FULL SHOT   FAVORING ABE IN BACKGROUND
> *As Gannon half-rises into shot, Abe, who had grabbed a heavy hunting knife, rushes forward and sinks it into Gannon's hand, but the shot is cut a few frames (perhaps one-tenth of a second) before it reaches his hand.*

CLOSE GROUP SHOT   GANG MEMBERS
> *They react to the o. s. action as the SOUND indicates knife being driven into the table top, and Gannon's SCREAM suggests it has been driven through his hand.*

Incidentally, in neither of these major scenes (1 and 3) were the cuts, as finally shot and edited, suggested in the script. If so, they wouldn't have been the censor's problem. They were improvised on the set. Free of any censorial problems, their effect was certainly less gruesome but, because the viewer had to bring his own emotions to the scene as shot, it was more involving, suspenseful, and effective than the version read by Shurlock. (None of the cuts showed Gannon's hand pinned to the table but every viewer knew it was there.)

Chapter Fifteen

Let us be honest. Memory is a camera whose lens is covered by a burlap filter and spattered with mud. Reality recalled is reality revised, refined, and reconstituted. As for its depth of vision, events that occurred months, sometimes years, apart jitter like vagrant molecules and displace each other.

With this in mind, the fourth decade of the 20th century is best viewed as a whole. Beginning before 1930 with the partial liberation of picture and sound, it progressed steadily both technologically and artistically to reach a triumphal climax in the wonder year of 1939. There were subtractions and additions; some famous names, unable or unwilling to cope with the demands of the new medium, quietly faded out of the Hollywood scene, but a surprising number of silent headliners, among them Greta Garbo, Myrna Loy, William Powell, and Mary Astor made successful transitions to sound. With steadily-increasing frequency, as the film medium grew from a stepchild of the theater to preeminence in the dramatic arts and acting in the movies was no longer a come-down, actors of all ages and reputations arrived in Hollywood to fill the needs of an expanding industry. The cinema had become a challenge which most theatrically-trained artists now eagerly faced.

In a number of ways Hollywood's triumph spelled trouble for Broadway. A young player needed only one good show in New York to earn a one-way ticket to Southern California, which left a skimpy roster of juveniles and ingénues for the theater. The stockpile of gifted dramatists slowly dwindled until, by the early '40s, only two or three established playwrights still wrote regularly for live audiences. As with actors, one Broadway success

119

was all that was needed to trigger Hollywood's siren call, whose ambiguous definition was completely ignored by those with stars in their eyes.

It can be reasonably argued that many promising careers, or established careers for that matter, were nipped in the bud or in mid-bloom by dreams of riches and wider reputations. (And this is as good a place as any to discuss that seeming contradiction as well as other traumas caused by a head-on collision of artist and the milieu which the disappointed, the defeated, and the envious call Tinseltown.)   Hollywood eclecticism was a reef that sank a number of avaricious artists.

It is a truism that good art comes from the gut-feelings of good artists, and their power to create rests on the talent to evoke and interpret their message with originality and empathy. The wise authors wrote about that which they felt, recognized, and tried to understand, yet I have known more than one writer who, having achieved success and a high earning potential by writing out of his deep-seated sensibilities, proceeded to lose his reputation and his good name by greedily grabbing the highest offers, whether or not they involved concepts with which he empathized.

Many of Hollywood's literary invaders failed to recognize that the writing of a film scenario was a craft in its own right. With few exceptions even hit plays were rewritten for the screen, usually not by the original play writes. It can be said flatly that most novelists, as well as some first-class playwrights, were not at ease with the unique dramatic structure of the screenplay—Odets, Irwin Shaw, Aldous Huxley, and Raymond Chandler immediately come to mind. Most writers who found the work uncomfortable or spiritually unfulfilling soon quit the scene; the unfortunate few who had cut all ties with their pasts sank into a morass of their own making. The playwrights among them inevitably wrote a play or two shifting the blame for their failures to the town's producers, its untalented directors, its seductive enticements, and its penchant for corrupting the honest artist. There were, of course, heartless producers and untalented directors in plenty, but Hollywood, then and now, never corrupted an artist who didn't knowingly welcome corruption. One had only to say an occasional "No!" to incompatible projects, no matter how prodigious the salary. The truly successful, both artistically and financially, have always done just that.

However, artists have shared their shortcomings with their less-talented brothers and sisters for many lifetimes; only the insentient aspects of society change from generation to generation, and any second-rate seer with good

The Carpetbaggers: Alan Ladd, Carole Baker and George Peppard

Carpetbaggers, wardrobe approval by director. Starting with star, Carol Baker, clockwise is designer Edith Head, presenting her sketches to Joe Levine, Marty Rackin and Eddie Dmytryk with his cameraman Joe MacDonald behind him.

hindsight could have predicted the evolution of motion-picture technology. Example: Most cameras had been equipped with electric motors long before sound's takeover and, outside of donning soundproof overcoats, they remained much the same for years to come; for perfect registration the old Mitchel is still hard to beat. The camera lens had been ground to near perfection and the film it exposed predated motion pictures. Their continued development moved at a random rate that ignored the contributions of other fields. Film grain was reduced and sensitivity to light increased in quantum leaps which, in turn, led to a greater use of mazda lighting and far less dependence on the blinding rays of the kliegs or the sun-arcs; that is until color, a prodigious light eater, arrived on the scene.

It is deceptive to say color "arrived." Just as sound had been hovering on the fringe since Edison, primitive color had been seen on the screen as early as 1906, though not to anyone's satisfaction. However, in another sense, usable color had been with us for years, disguised as tinted stock.

Almost all the film I had run as a projectionist was printed on tinted film, which had been available in quantity since before *The Birth of a Nation*. Exotic hand coloring had preceded tint, but it was too laborious, too uncertain, and too expensive for general use. On the other hand, tinted stock cost little more than black and white, required no extra laboratory treatment, did not detract from the reality of the scene, and was welcomed by the viewer. In short order it was a must for every feature film.

Camera slates carried a slot for color. "Straw" meant the scene should be printed on straw-tinted positive stock, the color for most exterior day scenes. 'Blue' was reserved for night exteriors, while amber was the choice for interior scenes lit by candles, lamps, or chandeliers. Red was the obvious color for fire scenes, and sepia was mandatory for deserts, and occasionally to establish mood. Raoul Walsh's *The Wanderer* was tinted a pale lavender sepia throughout its length. A two-tone wash of pink and blue was also available, but that was a lab job, not a tinted stock.

That appealing convention received its coup de grace from that epoch terminator, sound. Its striations on film required a clear base, and tint colored the entire frame, so it was banished from the medium. By the time the sound strip was cleared of dyes, full color had been perfected on a laminated film base, the superior three-strip film was in the wings, and Eastman, Pathe, et al. were out of the tint business.

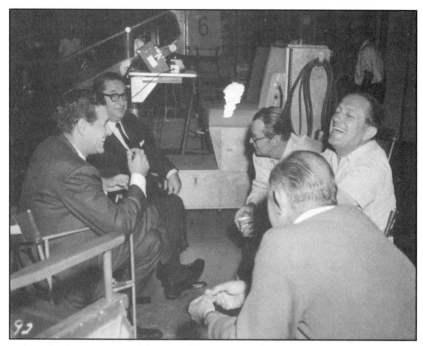

A production meeting on *The Carpetbaggers* 1963 with Marty Rackin and Joe Levine. "Sometimes there are laughs."

Double emulsion color film had been in development since the turn of the century, but none was economical or satisfactory, though DeMille used the color for biblical sequences in *The Ten Commandments* (1923). Herbert Kalmus, the founder of Technicolor, had been working on two-strip color since 1912, and in 1926 his perseverance paid off. Douglas Fairbanks considered it good enough to use for *The Black Pirate*.

Three-strip Technicolor was first used in Lloyd Corrigan's musical short, *La Cucaracha*, in 1933. It was enthusiastically received, and its next appearance was in Mamoulian's *Becky Sharp* (1935). From then on it was a case of, "When can we get it?" and "Who do you know?" and "Be very nice to Natalie Kalmus!" Parceled out carefully and, some thought, preferentially, it was used primarily for outdoor films and big musicals.

Technicolor was very expensive and, because it split light three ways to impact on three film strips, it was back to sun-arcs once more. The hot lighting and Technicolor's printing process produced an effect that was often garish or "postcardy." But COLOR was what the company was selling and the word "pastel" was forbidden within its walls. Moreover, since it was a worldwide monopoly it was always a "do it our way or forget it" deal. Yet on The Trail of the Lonesome Pine *Henry Hathaway succeeded in outwitting the company's color consultant by insisting that his mountain shacks, inside and out, be constructed of aged barn siding and that his actors be dressed in dull browns and blues. With the help of nature's dark-green pines he scored a perfect ten. But it was a long time before he got another commitment from Technicolor.*

The last major film to use the three-strip process was *The Caine Mutiny*, filmed in 1952-53.

We were shooting in the waters off Hawaii, and I had set up the camera on the foredeck of our destroyer, which was just back from the Korean front. I wanted to film a few salvos from the ship's main guns (more properly rifles). We got the skipper's "ready" sign, I rolled the camera, gave the signal to start, and waited. And waited The three-strip camera was grinding out 270 feet of useless film per minute, but the guns were mute. I waved my arms frantically toward the bridge, hoping to stop all action. I shouldn't have worried. Then I cut the camera and reslated. The skipper reported there had been a foul-up (surprise) and assured me that everything was now A-Okay—he was ready to go.

I crossed my fingers. On my signal to the bridge there was one shot, then silence—no salvo. On the third try we finally made it, and I realized that if this had been the real thing we would have been blown out of the water by now. I turned to our naval adviser, Lt. Commander Shaw.

"Commander," I asked, "how did we ever beat the Japanese?"

"They made more mistakes than we did," he answered, without a smile. In those days, the navy had no fear of the truth.

The Europeans had led the search for viable sound and color, but American developers were first to hit both jackpots. They were, indeed, worth the figurative one million dollars. And that led to interesting reactions abroad.

Just as sound was beginning to find its legs the world stumbled into the Great Depression. Money was scarce, the exchange was unfavorable and sound equipment for both studio and theater was controlled by a crafty Uncle Sam who saw not only profits, but a way to standardize the industry around the globe—to his yardstick, of course. The Europeans chose the only way out, a long, unhurried transition to sound. Would it had been slower.

Lt. Maryk (Van Johnson) calls to the pilothouse the officers of his ship to inform them that
he has relieved Capt. Queeg during the typhoon of The Stanley Kramer Production of
The Caine Mutiny for Columbia. Left to right: Arthur Franz, Bogart, Johnson, Todd Karnes,
David Albert, Robert Francis and Fred MacMurray. Edward Dmytryk is the director. 1954.

While Hollywood was turning out 100% talkies, which barely moved,
the Europeans (England excepted) were concentrating on images to minimize the theatricality of too much dialogue. Their camera techniques and
their blocking remained fluid, their photography expressive, and their
sound was used to enhance rather than elucidate the scene. In short, it
was an innovative and refreshing style. For instance:

Alexander Dovzhenko's Aerograd *(1935) dramatizes the building of a new
city in the Soviet Union's new society somewhere in the depths of Siberia. Suddenly one sequence breaks free of the obligatory propaganda; a worker is accused
of treachery, tried by his fellows, and condemned to death, the penalty to be
carried out by two of his friends. Stoically accepting his fate the condemned man
leads his reluctant executioners away from the sprouting city and into a glade at
the foot of a rocky escarpment. As his friends ready their rifles, he looks around at
the tranquil scene. For the last time he sees the quaking birch trees, hears the*

songs of the birds, and feels the soft wind on his cheek. Then, lifting his eyes to the sky, he opens his mouth and breaks the mood with a hair-raising scream—not a scream of fear, but an expression of the lusty life still in him. As the searing scream resounds through the glade, the executioners fire their guns and he falls to the ground. His life ebbs away with the dwindling echoes. Now there is only silence; even the wind has stopped blowing.

As I recall it, not one word was spoken during the whole episode. But once more a few pictures and one clear call for responsiveness was worth a thousand words—dramatically for those who wanted to see, viscerally for those who wanted to feel, and philosophically for those who wanted to search.

Yes, it was innovative and refreshing, but it died aborning, not because of sound, and not solely because of the Depression, but because the Russian revolution and the punitive peace treaty of Versailles created a time that was definitely out of joint. Adding to that heavy load was the weight of words. The Soviet Union and Germany, the two countries with the greatest potential for recreating the art of the motion picture labored under dictatorial restrictions much more demoralizing than the poverty of the depression.

While Franklin Roosevelt was informing and uplifting the American people with his Fireside Chats, the Soviet Union and Germany were clobbering their citizens with heavy-handed propaganda. Although their aims might have varied, all governments recognized the need to reach the people, but the dictatorial nations (including Italy, whose films were inconsequential) were the only governments to use the power of film to brainwash and imprint the huge number of their citizens who visited the movie theaters. And though in Russia Eisenstein and Dovzhenko developed symbolism obscure enough to fool the government censor, it also fooled the people and they soon closed up shop in despair.

In Berlin a few directors struggled to retain their integrity, but there, too, it was a hopeless fight. Once more propaganda films and powerful documentaries won the day, if not the public, and great directors like Murnau, Lang, and DuPont exiled themselves to California.

France had no problem with dictators, but the Depression and its related financial restrictions drove most of their established film companies out of business. Filmmakers had nowhere to turn. But poverty is a great spur to the creativity of those who won't give up, and the French soon patched together a new film hierarchy. Since company financing was no longer available, filmmakers were forced to become entrepreneurs and operators, and each filmmaker had to borrow, beg, or marry money to finance his new film. The end result was the establishment of a producer class which, unlike its counterpart in Hollywood, concerned itself solely with the procurement of the needed money. That done, the responsibility for all activities relating to the making of the film, from the writing of the script through production to the point of release, devolved on the director. In other words, he had full artistic control; and that's how "auteurs" were born. This method of production was the opposite of America's institutionalized film practices.

In the United States the film companies were in command, and although the studios were nominally autonomous in production matters, at times the final decision on whether some particular film should be made came from the front office in New York. If a filmmaker wished to make a special film, something beyond the product he was asked to turn out as a contract director, he had to sell the people in command. But if an agreement was reached, he knew the needed money was available and where it was coming from; financing was never a problem with the studio system. The filmmaker might have to compromise on leading players, since the studio's guarantee of a reasonable return was in their box office power, but beyond that the director was in control as long as he didn't go too far beyond his budget. (Schedule is always a hope rather than a reality, and means little outside of its relation to the budget.)

Occasionally independents tried to finance their films in the French manner, but distribution and exhibition were completely under the control of the de facto studio cartel, which at the time comprised the fourth-largest industry in the country.

Three of Hollywood's top directors, Wyler, Stevens, and McCarey formed an independent company, Liberty Films. I don't know about the other two, but McCarey, wanting to be totally free of studio input, hoped to get his own financing.

With this in mind he arranged an appointment with a leading Los Angeles bank that frequently lent money to the studios. McCarey presented his best pitch to a stony-faced financier. As he finished, the executive hemmed.

"Mr....McCarey...? I know what a cameraman does—he photographs the picture. I know what actors do—they play the parts. I know a writer writes the scenario. But tell me, Mr....uh...McCarey, what does a director do?"

Leo decided a touch of studio input was sufferable. He made a deal with a major company.

In another of Hollywood's contradictions a director could, once in a while, make his dream film if he had a solid relationship with the studio brass. Hollywood's few top directors with a proven record at the box office and with the critics could, to a carefully limited extent, write their own rules. Their main differences with the studio heads concerned the kind of picture to be made, rather than how to make it.

It is perhaps apocryphal, but it is truly illustrative. In John Ford's best years it was common knowledge that Hollywood's most revered director had an unwritten agreement with the several studios he worked for. Succinctly, it was: "I'll make two for you if you let me make one for myself." Even if that particular story was not quite true, it was a fact that more than one director had some such understanding. And it should not be considered remarkable that their visions, overall, proved no better than those of the studios.

There was one other way to make a film of one's choice. A special aspect of the Golden Age was that every major studio turned out fifty to sixty features each year, most of them all-out attempts at pleasing everybody. But a fast-talking director or producer could, on occasion, convince a studio production chief that a film he wanted to make would, successful or not, add to the studio's prestige. The word "prestige," skillfully used, was magic to the executive who had suffered the polite contempt of the artists of the theater in earlier days and *The New Yorker* magazine perpetually, and each studio was good for two or three prestige pictures per year. There were enough pleasant surprises to keep the practice alive.

In 1930 Universal Studios released two films (among many others): The King Of Jazz, *a big musical starring Paul Whiteman, who led the world's most popular big band, and* All Quiet On The Western Front, *starring nobody. The King Of Jazz was planned and promoted as the money film for 1930;* All Quiet *was Universal's prestige picture and a tax write-off.*

Lewis Milestone and All Quiet On The Western Front *won Academy Awards for Best Director and Best Picture and, in this instance, the prestige picture was able to make up the losses of* The King Of Jazz. *As they say in Hollywood, "Go figure!"*

CHAPTER SIXTEEN

Marcel Pagnol was France's Beauty as well as Beast. While the studios were going broke and the filmmakers were crying doom and disaster, their hopes were kept alive by the financially-successful transplantation of his popular plays to the screen. At the same time, in true Gallic style, he was castigated by French cinema lovers and critics for transferring the stage, almost intact, to celluloid, sans movement, sans imagery, sans those metaphoric elements which had transformed films into an independent art form, sans everything but words.

Not at all disturbed by his critics, he grew rich enough to buy his own studio in Marseilles, where he continued to make more of the same. And though in the late '50s some fine French directors tried to break the mold with the *Nouvelle Vague*, their success was short-lived. In the end some of the top directors sought refuge in America, but even here, with the exception of Louis Malle, they found the problems of the Hollywood process even more difficult than those they had left behind.

Hollywood was still two or three generations short of "casting" American presidents, but the medium it had helped spawn was fast becoming the world's most popular and most influential vehicle of entertainment, information, and change. Although this is meant to be a casual history of Hollywood in the Golden Age, foreign production which, paradoxically, helped to establish America's position at the top of the heap, should not be ignored. And the chief role in the acceleration of the rift between Hollywood's product and the rest of the world was played by the French.

Their films, on the whole, were too intellectual!

At the start of World War II Edward R. Murrow advised his radio reporters to use a broadcasting style that "could be understood by the truck driver, yet not insult the intellectual." (That rather loose quotation now raises politically correct questions about truck drivers and intellectuals, but this is not the arena for a sociological debate.)

In films that style was developed gradually, instinctively by some and consciously by others, when it was perceived that the language of the theater, which could veer from the poetic to the philosophic, was not welcomed by the mass public. The serious theater played almost exclusively to literate and aware audiences, whereas American films, which always aimed at a world market, tried to reach people of all intellectual and social levels.

Filmmakers who knew how to appeal to "everyman" and could, like Dovzhenko, create vivid images and metaphors had a head start in the formation of a divergent art. Dialogue, of course, could not be ignored, but because of the non-stop nature of film, which allows only an instant for the parsing of an obscure word or phrase, immediate recognition by all was an inescapable requirement.

The two-fold solution to the problem was easier to find than to apply. Since most actions and reactions are understood by people throughout the world without the need for translation, the first prescription called for less talking and more doing. But most screen writers are wordsmiths who find it easier to project their thoughts with words than with action, however slight, and many scripts were written in master scenes of dialogue only. (The practice persists to this day.) And since not too many directors are capable of reinterpreting talk into action, dialogue carried the ball.

In 1938 I was editing a film for one of Hollywood's best-known directors. At one point, the equally-famous leading lady found a line of dialogue "uncomfortable." A word or two would have solved the problem, but the director, perhaps because of his theatrical conditioning, would not risk his neck. A call was put in for the scriptwriter, an elderly woman who lived in Pasadena. Since she did not drive, a studio limousine was sent to fetch her. The two-way trip took well over an hour and, once on the set, she took a look at the offensive line, changed a few words, and left for Pasadena. The actress was happy, the director was relieved, and the crew and I could only wonder. The change could have easily been made by the star, the director, or on the telephone at the cost of a dime.

With Stanley Kramer &? Navy Chief technical advisor, Fred MacMurray, Van Johnson, Humphrey Bogart. *The Caine Mutiny*, 1953. This set was built on a stage at Columbia Studio to match interior of actual navy ship used in *The Caine Mutiny*.

Since the presence of a large number of words was inevitable the second and more workable solution was to find the most effective way to deal with dialogue, and Hemingway had blazed the trail before the movies talked. His basically Anglo-Saxon, monosyllabic words were quickly grasped and easily understood, and his working vocabulary (except for his foreign place names) was not too abstruse for any man or woman; yet as per Morrow's prescription, it was accepted by the most erudite of readers or viewers. Of course ambiguity, which is inherent in the English language, was a recurring annoyance, but that was not too difficult to deal with.

However, it was not exactly easy; another writer's problem was, and is, literary usage. In most tongues, including English, literary convention rarely duplicates common speech. A prewritten lecture sounds quite different from one spontaneously conceived and delivered. It may be more precise, certainly more formal, but as a rule it will not be as warm, as entertaining, as in tune with the audience as a discourse delivered extemporaneously by an artist of ad-lib.

Since nearly all writers learn much of their craft by reading, transplanted writing conventions are usually deep-set and well-protected. An Italian friend of mine told me he was effectively estranged from many of his colleagues when he began to write in the vernacular. But "literary style" is firmly entrenched in all languages, and one has only to read some English dialogue aloud to recognize that much of it does not smack of the street or the living room, and even the "real" dialogue of Ernest Hemingway has a stylized ring.

To a decent extent, however, the better scripts that have been written by the better writers, or rewritten by directors who are good "play doctors," sound eminently human. In either case, an ear for speech in all its forms is imperative; fifty-year-old films that had the advantage of such writers and directors still live today. And actors who have freed themselves from a slavish dependence on the written word can exercise an equal influence.

While shooting Broken Lance, *I had studied a long speech in a scene Spencer Tracy was scheduled to do in a day or two. It was stiff and "literary." After reworking it I showed it to Tracy, but he barely glanced at it.*

"Eddie," he said, "I've already worked on that one, and I'd like to do it as is. If you don't like it, I'll do your version."

Two days later we shot the scene. Tracy spoke the scripted lines—but hardly "as is." He hemmed, he hawed, he stuttered, repeated words, even phrases. In short, he broke it up in such a way that it became a completely spontaneous utterance of a man who was thinking it out on the spot. And no one would have recognized it as the speech from the script. Spence had spoken the lines not as I had read them, but as I wished I had been able to read them.

But that was Tracy's incomparable art; he played with words the way Louis Armstrong played with tunes and lyrics. Each improved the original material, which is what one should expect from the great artists in all the performing arts.[37]

Of course, even with the best of intentions there is an occasional 'glitch.' I stopped one of Tracy's scenes in the middle of a take, something I did rarely. He looked at me in surprise.

"Why?" he asked.

"Because," I said, "you were hemming and hawing a little too much." Tracy drew himself up to his full height.

"Young man," he announced, "I get paid a great deal of money for hemming and hawing!"

He said it with a wry grin, but he was telling the truth. However, in the next take he brought it down to reality.

Like those mythical beings who could change form in the blink of an eye, motion pictures have many shapes and many faces. It depends on what a person with a little money in the bank, a film or TV camera at his command, and a great deal of arrogance in his character wants to "show and tell." Although it may pain a cinematic purist, a film can be a travelogue, a documentary, a biography, an opera, a ballet, a nature film, a sermon or its equivalent, propaganda, or any number of other forms that offer entertainment and/or information.

The truth is that most of these cinematic branches were sponsored or subsidized, just as many of the fine arts are today. That truth stretched far enough to include feature films, for almost every country except the United States subsidized its home production with money grants or Quota Acts aimed at Hollywood pictures. France certified only a small number of American films for distribution, and Britain, while rewarding those Hollywood companies that spent a great deal of their budgets in England, established a quota on the number of American films that could be shown in British film houses. In both cases, homemade films were subsidized to fill the gaps.

The looming shadow of World War II was a major factor in Hollywood's final conquest of the world market, but aside from the fact that its films were exuberant in a time of universal Depression, optimistic in a time of despair, and moved at a pace that bypassed boredom, there was one more element in its drive for supremacy—an accommodation with art.

The better European films were made by the literati for the literati, while Hollywood was turning out well-fashioned pictures for everyone. The Europeans discussed or dramatized love, war, politics, and family matters articulately in slow moving scenes of endless talk, often too sophisticated, too esoteric, or too recondite for their own man-in-the-street; Hollywood presciently followed Ed Murrow's recipe and delivered the same subjects in language easily understood, easily dubbed, and spoken by actors of international repute. Given the choice between Henri-Georges Clouzot and Jean Cocteau or Raoul Walsh and Howard Hawks, the average European would have picked either of the latter. It would have been no contest.

CHAPTER SEVENTEEN

Ages and Eras can usually be dated without recourse to approxima-tion, and it is only necessary to strip away the patina of nostalgia laid down by the passage of time to see that any golden age is created by the blood, sweat, and tears of inspired men and women, for genius does not come easily. Although Hollywood's Golden Age is too recent to be fixed with absolute accuracy, film scholars will almost certainly agree that Griffith's *The Birth of a Nation* (1915), was the film marking the movies' earliest sign of maturation, and the start of a new era. The first motion picture to alert the world to the medium's potential for greatness, it had within it the seeds, and some buds, of all that film would one day be-come; all, that is, except a voice and a civilized concept. The voice arrived some twelve years later, and the concept…? It sprouted in the '30s, flow-ered in the '40s, then, with rare exceptions, withered with the adultera-tion of the era.

In 1926, one of the world's great scientists had predicted the newly-born talking picture would die in infancy, but in just a dozen years it reached the apex of a robust development. In those few years the medium matured into the world's most popular and most dynamic art form; whether it was the best is a question of taste, but if a worldwide consensus had been called for in 1939, film would have had no opposition worthy of the name.

From 1926 through 1938 the crude ore of the Golden Age was shaped and polished by a host of creative men and women; actors from the the-ater, successful graduates of the silents, novelists, short-story writers, play-

135

wrights, and journalists worked with producers of quality but, as it has often been said, "film is a director's medium." Since I earned my director's chair in 1939, I openly confess a bias in the matter, and it is this group of artists I choose to spearhead the triumphs of the '30s.

Reinvigorated by the mind-blowing challenges of the proliferating art, the outstanding directors of the period—the leaders of the pack—nursed their "flicks" into "cinema." A review of the record will show it is almost exclusively a triumph of the old timers who were still in their prime. Between 1927 and 1939 the Academy Awards for the best direction were won by Frank Borzage (twice), Lewis Milestone (twice), Frank Lloyd (twice), Frank Capra (three times), Norman Taurog, John Ford, Leo McCarey, and Victor Fleming. Ford went on to win three more awards in the '40s, McCarey another, and George Stevens and Willie Wyler were soon to have their days.

At the 1937 Academy Awards presentations Leo McCarey stepped up to the podium to receive his Oscar for the best direction of the year on The Awful Truth. *Like many of his colleagues Leo was somewhat shy and, as was his custom, he had fortified himself with liquid courage. He accepted the statuette, then turned to the audience.*

"The Awful Truth," he said, "is not the best picture I made last year."

The audience didn't know whether to gasp or laugh, so it did both. Only a few remembered that McCarey had also made Make Way For Tomorrow *in 1936. And though Paramount's exhibitors would have voted it the box office disaster of the year, this story of the elderly was Leo's favorite film.*

The Oscar-winning directors of the decade represented only a segment of the front ranks; as previously noted, the Academy has a reputation for overlooking some of the town's greatest talents, an incongruity that testifies to its truly democratic voting process. King Vidor, Lubitsch, Mamoulian, Howard Hawks, Gregory LaCava, Archie Mayo, Raoul Walsh, Allen Dwan, Clarence Brown, and several others were quite at home in the top echelon. With the exception of Mamoulian these men, as well as the award-winners, all learned their trade in silent films, and many were top contributors for the next two decades.

Strange to say, few of the European directors who arrived in Hollywood after the advent of sound achieved success in the '30s, and the best of them were the most likely to fail. In spite of his international reputation, the extent of Sergei Eisenstein's failure is an outstanding case in point.

In 1930 Paramount brought him to Hollywood, where he spent months sparring with the studio over subject matter, a classic instance of the intellectual (Eisenstein) versus the common man (Paramount) approaches. They finally reached an agreement on Dreiser's An American Tragedy, *but Eisenstein's script met a quick and total rebuff. Unable to crack the studios, he managed to get financial backing from Upton Sinclair for a film,* Que Viva Mexico, *to be made south of the border. However, the free enterprise system could not cope with the mindset of an artist accustomed to 100% government support; Eisenstein spent dollars as if they were kopecks, rejected financial supervision, and drained Sinclair and his co-investors dry. Eventually he retreated to a cool welcome in the Soviet Union while a complete miscarriage,* Thunder Over Mexico, *was edited out of the miles of film he left behind.[38]*

The Making and Unmaking of 'Que Viva Mexico,' edited by Harry M. Geduld and Ronal Gottesman, discloses, intentionally or not, a problem which defeated many foreign directors; whether they came from communist societies, which doled out minimum wages to all, or from European countries whose labor costs were low enough to make schedules an unnecessary nuisance, most alien 'auteurs' found their talents stifled by the demands of Hollywood production practices at least as much as by their different approaches to content and substance.

On a large weed-filled lot just inside the gates of the DeLaurentis Film Studio stood a lofty set. It had been built for a Fellini film perhaps a year before I arrived on the lot. As the story goes, Fellini came out, accompanied by his working entourage, sat in the sun for a day or two contemplating the structure, decided it failed to inspire him, walked away and never came back. But the set remained, isolated and weatherworn, a monument to a stillborn dream, a broken deal, and an auteur's whim.

A year later, at the same studio, I was making Anzio. *When "ferragosto," the long holiday that empties the streets of Rome for two or more weeks in August and early September arrived, Dino decided to close the studio for the duration.*

"Can you afford the carrying costs?" I asked.

"What costs!" It was a statement, not a question. "You and the cast," he continued, "are under contract and well within the time limits. As for the

crew…" He made one of those dismissive gestures that only a Neapolitan can manage. *"I make a profit by shutting the studio down for a few days."*

And that was in 1967. In the '30s, with European labor costs even lower, that was undoubtedly an ideal solution in Italy, but Hollywood crewmen were the most highly-paid workers in the world and the studios had, to a great extent, eliminated such budget-busting moratoria, often at the cost of the services of the auteurs who indulged in them.

Several British and Continental directors of the second class, accustomed to scraping the bottom of the barrel for their productions, had little trouble adjusting to the Hollywood system. But the self-indulgent behavior of Europe's autocratic auteurs did little to win the cooperation of the studio brass or the freewheeling American crews who responded best to leaders rather than dictators. Most of them returned home blaming the system for their failures. Which leads to a parenthetical paragraph.

(Foreign film folk and many American "experts," with no studio experience believed that, compared to the auteur practices in Europe, Hollywood directors were under the thumbs of executives and producers. The belief bears no resemblance to the truth. Hollywood's best directors, even when the studios reigned supreme, always enjoyed full freedom, at least as long as that freedom was used to create and not to bludgeon.)

Henry Hathaway was a charming and friendly man when off the set, but a notoriously demonic Mr. Hyde while shooting (nerves, of course). Occasionally his imagination was as uncontrollable as his temper, and his obstinacy, which grew in direct proportion to the silliness of some of his creations, made things difficult for those who worked with him.

In 1936 Henry was filming Souls At Sea, *and had arrived at the film's furious climax—a sequence of panic on a sinking schooner caught in a hurricane. Now hurricanes are neither safe nor easily available for controlled shooting, so the sequence was being staged in the studio's tank whose mechanically-created waves were augmented and enhanced by the wild oceanic turbulence projected onto the giant process screen in the shot's background. A pivotal story action required Gary Cooper to dive into the heaving waters, and the Muse of creativity smiled on Henry—or so he thought.*

Hathaway had noticed that the photographed waves on the process screen looked more "hairy" than the rolling water movement in the tank, and he

Montomery Clift and Dean Martin in *The Young Lions*, 1957.

Marlon Brando in *The Young Lions*, 1957.

suddenly decided that Cooper should dive head first into the mountainous waves on the screen. All that stood in his way was the common sense of Farciot Eduard, Paramount's process genius, who pointed out that such a dive might put a hole in Gary's pate, and most certainly one in his costly screen, as well as putting the set out of commission for a number of days.

Hathaway thundered, but Farciot was in control of his temper and the process equipment; he refused to run the background scene. To decide the issue Henry dragged Farciot to the top, which meant the studio chief, Bill LeBaron. Unfortunately for Hathaway, the unimaginative LeBaron instantly recognized the logic of Farciot's position, as well as the danger to the head of one of the studio's leading stars; he ruled against Henry and for sanity.

To my knowledge this was one of the very few times a top executive was involved in a creative decision during the shooting of a film. Considering the field as a whole, would it had happened more often.

Men like Capra, Stevens, Wyler, Lubitsch, Milestone, and other top film-makers were able to control their own scripts, select their own crews and casts (with a minimal amount of compromise on 'star' values), supervise the dubbing, and often take part in the distribution and exhibition planning. As for the director's cut, seldom did a top director have to fight producers or executives about editing. Although differences of opinion occasionally led to moderate compromises, in my experience these were rare indeed.

This mini-sidebar has been somewhat aggravated by the rise of the restorers, who (I believe unwittingly) have given voice to a good deal of nonsense about the superiority of their "fully restored" films. If one considers only the physical aspects of their films, their claim is well founded, but they are more often wrong than right in their replacement of scenes and sequences excised from the director's cut. To begin with, not too many directors are skilled film editors, while others, as mentioned earlier, fall in love with their work to the extent of losing their ability to make unbiased judgments. Moreover, excisions are often made at the director's request.

An example of a rather misguided restoration is the Judy Garland version of *A Star Is Born*. Although the improvement of the physical qualities of the film—color, grain, sound, et al.—make it a valuable contribution to the living history of Hollywood and the screen, the restoration of excised scenes is another matter. Two deleted musical numbers restored to an already longish film in no way helped the overall quality or viewer appeal. In plain words, they were dull and uninspiring additions, far inferior to those retained in the

Directing Elizabeth Taylor in *Raintree County*, 1956.

studio cut. In one of them Miss Garland looks her age rather than that of an ingénue in her early twenties that the story calls for, and I believe the director, George Cukor, was probably among the first to ask for the number's deletion.

The same can probably be said for director's cuts in a large number of instances, for rarely did a director with a well-developed sense of artistic responsibility find a producer or a studio executive looking over his shoulder. They had chores of their own to take care of.

Y. Frank Freeman was the production head of Paramount for a longer tenure than most. He took an eclectic interest in the studio's activities, and one fine day he decided to inspect the back lot. In one of its far recesses he spotted an elderly man sitting on a pile of salvaged lumber, smoking a cigarette.

"Aren't you supposed to be working?" asked Freeman.

"Yup," said the elderly man. Then he peered closely at his interrogator.

"Hey," he said, "aren't you Mr. Freeman?"

"Yup," said Y. Frank.

"Well," said the elderly man, "you get paid a hell of a lot more for running the studio than I get for pulling nails. Why aren't you taking care of your business?"

And Y. Frank Freeman, a decent man with a fine sense of humor and a sucker for logic, cut straight across the lot back to his office.

A pair of Teutonic directors whose talents transcended their less-likable cultural tendencies had a decided influence of Hollywood's filmmakers, in spite of their deceptively small Hollywood output.

Fritz Lang, an Austrian working in Germany, made two pictures of international quality: *Metropolis* (1927), an exceedingly cynical view of the

Fritz Lang's *M*.

world's future society, and *M* (1931), an unexcelled story of the pursuit and capture of a psychotic pedophile. Lang, whose mother had a Jewish background, left Berlin early in Hitler's reign and reached Hollywood in 1934. *Fury*, his first American film, was perhaps his best; a powerful study of lynching and mob violence, it antedated *The Ox-Bow Incident* by seven years. Although too far ahead of its time to score a box office success it had a marked effect on the sociocritical films of the '40s. In spite of confrontations with producers and executives over material and with actors who resented his dictatorial manner, Lang, who became an American citizen, managed a sporadic career through the '50s while concentrating on films of substance which benefited from his nonconformist views of American society. More than most Hollywood directors he had a talent for making his admonitory films dramatically diverting rather than preachy.

Topping Lang in technical creativity and with a more optimistic view of the world he lived in, Friedrich Murnau was one of the giants of the Golden Age. The triad of films on which his reputation rests, *Nosferatu* (1922), *The Last Laugh* (1924), and *Sunrise* (1927), marked the apex of the silent era. It is difficult if not impossible to name another director who made top-of-the-line films in three different genres.

The first of these, *Nosferatu, Eine Symphonie Des Grauens* or, more comfortably, *Nosferatu, The Vampire*, featuring the mythical Count Dracula, was realized in the expressionistic mode. It led the way for an unending string of fifth-rate macabriana, but it also foreshadowed Murnau's matchless talent for developing the potential of filmic language.

His next film, *The Last Laugh*, showed brilliant technical maturation. Whether or not he invented the dolly shot is debatable, but his use of the moving camera to bring life to what might otherwise have been a lethargic film was unparalleled at the time. His mood lighting (executed by cinematographer Karl Freund), his choice of sets and settings, and his set-ups, were without equal until *Citizen Kane*. (Orson Welles freely acknowledged his indebtedness to Murnau's influence.) Although the art of film-making has benefited from the contributions of many sources, a case can be made for Murnau as the greatest innovator and developer in film history. With the exception of D. W. Griffith, no other filmmaker could claim that honor. *The Last Laugh*, which was devoid of titles, and his last silent, *Sunrise*, served as blueprints for the better sound films of the future.

Murnau's third classic, *Sunrise* (1927), was his first Hollywood assignment; it was possibly the best film of the silent era. (It has also been acclaimed by some as the greatest motion picture ever made, but tastes vary with time and such evaluations never go unchallenged.) Murnau made two more films for Fox, but in March of 1931, at forty-one years of age, he lost his life in a manner befitting a dramatic genius.

Murnau's death was quite in keeping with the field to which he had made a notable contribution—the world of witchery. The story starts in Tahiti. It seems that while shooting Tabu he had violated a sacred Polynesian site believed to be guarded by a big black dog—an animal that appears in many of the world's mythologies. The local kahunas had warned him of the fate his skepticism might invite but oddly, in spite of his involvement in Tabu,

Nosferatu, and other films dealing with the supernatural, he refused to heed the warnings.

Back in Hollywood, just one week before the premiere of Tabu, *Murnau decided to visit Monterey. As his chauffeur told it, they were traveling at night along the Pacific Coast Highway when, somewhere between Ventura and Santa Barbara, a big black dog suddenly appeared in the car's headlights. In his efforts to avoid the animal he ran the car off the road and Murnau was killed in the ensuing crash. The chauffeur was uninjured, and no big black dog was ever found in that area. Where it came from and where it went remained a mystery, as did the intriguing tag.*

The captain of the first ship to reach Tahiti with news of Murnau's fatal accident discovered that the then-isolated community had known of the filmmaker's fate from the day of his death. And the big black dog was back guarding the defiled, but avenged, holy ground.

Unlike superstition, tradition is honored and admired, but it too often becomes a deterrent to progress. However, three score years ago our mongrel art was not yet hampered by orthodoxy, and Hollywood's filmmakers freely adapted European techniques. Reworking and blending them with their own, they arrived at a style that was loved by the world's film viewers even as it became a target for the barbs of the more conservative critics, which, for a popular art, is often more of a thumbs-up than a rap. And once more the men who led the way in establishing Hollywood movies as the cream of the crop were the veterans of the silent era.

Steeped in Keystone Kops comedy techniques, Frank Capra found the road that led to *Mr. Deeds Goes To Town* and *Mr. Smith Goes To Washington.* Using a mountain of two-reel Westerns as a springboard, Willie Wyler reached infinitely higher peaks with *Jezebel* and *Wuthering Heights.* And Leo McCarey, after creating the comedy formula that assured Laurel and Hardy lasting fame, displayed his talent for diversification which ranged from the hilarious buffoonery of *Duck Soup* to the sophisticated humor of *The Awful Truth.* No other Hollywood director had his talent for empathizing professionally with such varied personalities as W. C. Fields, Groucho Marx, Mae West, Bing Crosby, Ingrid Bergman, Cary Grant, Charles Boyer, Irene Dunne, and Charles Laughton.

Praying for the sun to stay out. Time is DOLLARS SPENT. In Rome, with *Anzio*, 1967.

Edward Dmytryk shooting *Anzio* in Rome with actor Robert Ryan.

Laughton—"Buster" to his friends—was a complete actor who could evoke a belly laugh with a single raspberry in If I Had A Million, *provoke a historical insurrection in* Mutiny on the Bounty, *and be convincing as a head-lopping sovereign in* Henry VIII *or the circumspect English butler in* Ruggles of Red Gap. *But Buster was also a ham.*

Not consciously, as most bad actors are, but inherently so. His Play-Doh cheeks, turgid lips, and swivelling eyeballs made almost any reaction an amplification. And since Laughton was an uninhibitedly sensitive man he managed a river of responses. The problem was that McCarey, who had an unusual ear for language and a surpassing ability to separate the pay dirt from the slag in any scene, was too wise to impose upon his actors' thespian skills which, he conceded, were greater than his own.

After seeing the first day's rushes I mentioned my misgivings about the caricatural quality of Laughton's reactions. McCarey used two fingers to simulate a working pair of scissors and I read the gesture as a blank check. From then on most of Laughton's overloaded takes wound up in the trims. (No, we don't leave film on the cutting room floor.) The unexpected climax of the matter came in a most dramatic scene.

"Ruggles," the British butler personified, becomes the property of a newly-rich, homespun Western character as the result of a poker bet. At one point while he, his boss, and some of his boss's friends are having a drink in a Colorado saloon, his boss essays a quotation from Lincoln's Gettysburg Address, but his memory fails him. The saloon's regulars, all good Americans, share his failing. Meanwhile, too shy to pipe up, Ruggles whispers to himself, "Four score and seven years ago..." His boss overhears him and, intrigued that an Englishman is more in touch with American history than he is, induces him to stand up and speak out, which he does. Quietly but effectively his voice picks up strength as his emotions mount. And that was the problem.

McCarey wished to film the speech in one perfect take, but Robert Burns' caveat, "The best-laid schemes of mice and men, etc...." should be engraved on every filmmaker's memory. Here the problem was not with the words, which are easily learned and spoken, but with the message. When Laughton arrived at "...and dedicated to the proposition that all men are created equal"—and that was just the end of the first sentence—his eyes are blinking away the tears that puddled up from the well of his emotions.

Hoping that reiteration might dull Laughton's sensitivities, McCarey kept shooting in fits and starts, but the battle for the perfect take was lost. Take after take was broken by sobs, by rolling eyes, by blubbering lips, and the

Directing Robert Mitchum night shots outside Rome. *Anzio*.

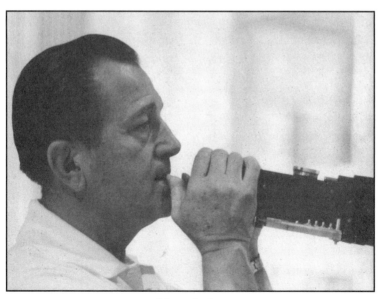

More *Anzio*.

Gettysburg Address refused to become routine. At the end of a day and a half of labor the actor, sobbing more in pain than emotion, dropped to his knees, threw his arms around Leo's legs, and begged him to stop the torture. McCarey, as emotionally spent as Laughton, was happy to acquiesce.

The speech was covered by some twenty-six incomplete segments, but fortunately a large part of the magic of motion pictures is the amazing sense of continuity and drama that can be achieved by the juxtaposition of dribs and drabs. Splicing together pieces of sound track, some only four or five inches long and encompassing a single word, others including a full line or more, added up to a complete and very satisfactory speech. However, matching synched images to the snippets of sound was clearly impossible. In the end the sequence contained three very short close shots of Laughton in his least emotional mode, a total of ten or twelve seconds during the two-minute address. The rest of the speech, in which Laughton was an invisible voice, was played over shots of the spellbound saloon habitués.

On viewing the finished cut prior to a sneak preview, Paramount's executive producer, who at the moment happened to be Ernst Lubitsch, suggested that as the film's star Laughton deserved more closeups in his big scene. McCarey agreed, and two more cuts of the star were included in the preview print.

The film, a gentle comedy, played beautifully until the Gettysburg Address, but when the first cut of the lugubrious Laughton appeared, the audience broke into raucous laughter, which continued throughout the rest of the scene whether or not he was on the screen.

Now a cardinal rule of comedy is that the viewer should laugh at the comedian's performance or character, but not at the comedian himself. One laughed at the trials and misadventures of Charlie, the little tramp, but never at Charles Spencer Chaplin. And although the Gettysburg Address was an integral part of an amusing scene, it was not meant to be laughed at.

Without waiting for the end of the film McCarey called me for a consultation in the men's room. "Put it back the way you had it," he said. So, of course, I did. At the next "sneak," without Laughton's woeful countenance to accompany his artful reading, the scene played to heightened interest but no laughter. But a lesson had been learned, for never had the catchphrase "One picture is worth a thousand words" so effectively revealed its flipside.

If one had to pick a single actor to epitomize the '30s, "Buster" would not be a bad choice. In that decade's films sentiment often reached the point of mawkishness, but when, like Laughton's unrestrained reactions,

"Director Edward Dmytryk, who made *The Young Lions* and many other great films, is dwarfed by one in marble as he awaits a lighting change during location filming of Anzio, Dino DeLaurentiis' spectacular battle epic starring Robert Mitchum. Dmytryk filmed a number of interior scenes for Anzio at the Royal Palace at Caserta, Italy. Columbia Pictures is releasing the Easmancolor-Panavission battle drama." 1967.

the awkward and the overdone were weeded out there remained a core of creativity and enough originality to obviate the need for sequels. However, as early as 1930 there were definite signs that the crossbreeding of theater and silent films had produced an evolutionary anomaly. Technical aspects such as freedom of movement and location, and the art of editing, which included the manipulation of the viewer's point of view and the intensity of the actors' reactions, were nudging films away from its parent art. But it was the acting style, which many assumed would bring movies completely into the theatrical fold, that underwent the most noticeable mutation of all, and created a problem for many writers and directors. For the actor had now become an important member of the creative team.

It didn't happen overnight. The first thing to go was "Wild Bill" Wellman's Kansas City British, as a few actors, especially those who had survived in spite of their lack of stage training, became convinced that motion picture viewers formed a class that considered it an unattractive, almost un-American affectation. And while "mugging" and orotund vocalization continued for a few more years, the more perceptive stage thespians began to see the light. Among the early converts was Spencer Tracy, who became the "prince of underplayers," not only vocally but also in the controlled use of body language and facial expression. Oddly enough, it was some time before filmmakers and movie buffs who had considered Tracy's screen restraint a gimmick to attract attention recognized it as an expression of acting honesty. To a large extent the increasing use of closeups, which magnified the slightest facial twitch into an undesirable tic, made acting moderation inevitable.

During the middle '30s Tracy got some heavy help from actors like Jimmy Stewart and Hank Fonda, and being a character rather than acting one soon became the goal of those actors gifted enough to handle the concept.[39] If this sounds like method acting, perish the thought. All three disdained the technique. Tracy and Bogart bridled at the mere mention of the phrase.

The difference between acting and being is difficult to elucidate. Simply, though inadequately stated, acting, no matter how skillfully accomplished, is an impersonation, but Tracy, for example, could make a viewer believe he was actually seeing a Portuguese fisherman, a Catholic priest, a Swiss mountain guide, or even the father of the bride, any of whom might *resemble* Spencer Tracy. And Humphrey Bogart will always be Captain Queeg. On the other hand, no matter how competently they interpreted their roles, actors like Clark Gable, John Wayne, and Marilyn Monroe were regarded as idols who overshadowed any character they might play.

We were on our way to Hong Kong and had stopped for a publicity layout in Japan. On our first evening in Tokyo we had been invited to one of the city's theaters that featured only women of all types and ages performing modern or classical dances. While watching a chorus line dancing in precise formation, a la New York City's Rockettes, I was tapped on the shoulder by the theater manager who whispered an invitation to visit the theater's star, a kabuki dancer. After traversing a number of backstage corridors where dozens of girls peeked out at the alien visitors and climbing four flights of stairs, we neared the star's dressing room. While the manager went in to announce our presence we waited outside. In a minute she stepped out, a tiny person clad in the long white traditional gown of her art. Her hair was dressed in classical style and her face was covered by a layer of chalk-white rice powder. She made no move as Gable held out his hand, she just looked up into his face as though she were beholding a god while tears traced two paths through the powder on her cheeks. And mind you, she was a star. But Gable was the King, even in Japan. And I was suddenly nowhere.

To return to the problem for writers and some directors created by changes in acting: Contrary to theater regulations a line in a script can be changed at the director's whim, and I have occasionally been asked by students how I get actors to read lines as I would like to hear them. My answer is, "I don't." At their surprised reaction, I explain, "How can I tell a Spencer Tracy or a Marlon Brando how to read a line?"

Reading lines is their business, their art, and if they can't say a line much better than I can, I wouldn't be using them in my film. For any director to ask a good actor to mimic his or her reading would be the height of idiocy.

Even the author of the screenplay should know—in fact, he should hope—that the actor will create modulations and nuances that will surprise and please him. How often have I and the rest of the crew stood entranced by the magic reality Spencer Tracy brought to a quite ordinary string of words. And how often have I and the rest of the crew "puddled up," not because of any sadness in the scene but for the perfection of his performance? It is one of the few immediate pleasures a director gets while shooting a film.

During the making of Raintree County *I was discussing a scene with Montgomery Clift and, quite inadvertently, I started to repeat one of the scene's lines. I had said only a few words when Monty put a hand on my knee.*

"Eddie," he said, "please don't read that line. You do it so beautifully you will inhibit me."

I must have turned red, since that was a mistake I rarely made. Then we both laughed. And to this day I can only paraphrase, not quote, a line from any script I have ever worked on.

By the end of the decade, not only acting but nearly every aspect of the film medium had changed remarkably. In some instances film techniques that had been sacrificed on the altar of embryonic sound resurfaced like the mythical phoenix. In others, techniques that owed their existence to sound were perfected, and by the end of 1938 films on the whole were as good as they were going to get. To substantiate this point of view, here are the ten nominees for the Academy's "Best Film of the Year" (awarded early in 1939). Many critics have judged them to be the greatest group of movies to grace the Golden Age.

Dark Victory	*Ninotchka*
Gone With The Wind	*Of Mice And Men*
Goodbye Mr. Chips	*Stagecoach*
Love Affair	*The Wizard Of Oz*
Mr. Smith Goes To Washington	*Wuthering Heights*

The winner, as almost everyone knows, was *Gone With The Wind*. It is still considered by many to be the greatest motion picture of all time.

Chapter Eighteen

The early '30s gave birth to the Bs—B as in good business, although that was not universally appreciated by studio workers who treated the low-budget flicks as if they were Cinderellas of the first part. Still, in hard times the Bs kept more than one studio afloat, and when they finally disappeared so did some of the studios.[40] Like Rodney Dangerfield, the Bs "got no respect"; critics ignored them while reviewers gave them grudging attention only when, as sometimes happened, they returned more profit per dollar spent than many of the As. But regardless of its quality, no B could fail—a happy condition guaranteed by the film companies' locked-in theaters.

At this date it is difficult to determine whether the practice of showing a second feature (a tactic designed to offset the effect of the Great Depression) gave rise to the Bs, or whether the production of Bs promoted the proliferation of second features, but it is almost too much to believe that the industry-wide concept was planned; it is far more likely that some haphazard action by some theater manager was responsible for the genesis of the practice.

Whatever its origin, its success was inevitable. Every producing company owned hundreds, some even thousands, of theaters, and each theater, regardless of its daily receipts, was assessed a flat price for the second feature, usually a B. The predetermined take of a company's chain of houses established the maximum budget allowable for the average B production to show a profit. Example: a Boris Karloff B made at Columbia garnered an assured studio share of $150,000.[41] Ergo the maximum budget for each of his films was set at around $100,000, and that, in turn, dictated a

Edward Dmytryk directing Boris Karloff in *The Devil Commands*.

shooting schedule of twelve days. The same formula was applied to the *Lone Wolf* series with Warren William and the *Boston Blackie* series starring Chester Morris. Each of the three stars was paid $15,000 per picture. RKO, which belonged in the Columbia category, made its Bs at approximately the same cost and on the same schedules.

Of course, most Bs were single features, but every studio had at least one series as part of its annual program. Paramount, for instance, produced the running adventures of *Bulldog Drummond*.

They were B versions of the Ronald Colman features made in '29 and '34, and starred John Howard as Drummond and John Barrymore as his relentless adversary. I edited one of the films in the series and discovered that even a B film could be the source of interesting company and occasionally a memorable experience. Perhaps the most enjoyable was playing the spelling game with Phi Beta Kappa key carrier John Howard and an amazingly sciolistic John Barrymore.

Playing broader rules than usual, we could add letters to either end of any word that could be found in the huge unabridged Webster's dictionary we kept on the stage. It was at one of these sessions that I first encountered the words "nargileh" and "sjambok," both offered by Barrymore. This was long before pot and a Desert Storm acquainted us with some of the less-admirable aspects of Arabic society, and I never found an occasion to casually drop the words into a conversation. But I have remembered them for more than half a century.

Barrymore, an intense, charming, but often gloomy man, was also a notorious non-bather. He changed into his film wardrobe on the set, and his own shirt, which he had probably worn through a bibulous night and through many such nights previously, sported a two-inch-wide ring-around-the-collar no miracle soap suds could have defeated. He had once been a newspaper cartoonist, and when we weren't playing the game he spent his free moments drawing anonymous portraits on any sheet of paper that came to hand, usually a page of the L. A. Times. He was an accomplished sketch artist, though his style challenged all of one's nonprofessional psychiatric lore. After drawing an excellent head he would energetically fill in all the clear spaces with heavy pencil strokes, turning a pleasant Dr. Jekyll into a ghoulish Mr. Hyde.

Barrymore made no secret of his heavy drinking, and though the studio hired a bodyguard to keep him away from alcohol throughout the eighteen day schedule, no escort outside a Raymond Chandler novel could match wits with a man who was comfortable with sjambok. Night work was always a gamble; he would float onto the set after dinner at Oblath's under a full head of booze. At such times he was too unfocused to read the lines on his cue card and his resulting self-anger was sad to see.

At this stage of his career this once-great actor, who could still declaim any Shakespearean speech with ease, could not remember two words from the script, but with Barrymore creativity he turned his weakness into an advantage. As he searched for his words on the cue card he conveyed the impression that he was looking off into space while thinking deeply about what he was hearing and saying. Nevertheless, because of his drinking-related unreliability, he was soon regarded as a clown.

Toward the end of his career he was a regular on the Orson Welles weekly radio show. His tongue was usually thick with drink and he was relegated to broad comedy skits where bumbling speech was no handicap. But now and then Wells would stage a scene from one of the Bard's plays in which Orson would play the lead, and because Barrymore was one of a very few actors who could make a Shakespearean character sound unpretentious, he would undertake an important supporting role. Miraculously, his voice would change, his words become clean, concise, unaffected, completely understandable and strangely touching (perhaps my reaction to his fleeting resurrection). Welles was to be admired for giving Barrymore such opportunities; he must have been aware that this superb artist, at least when such material was on the line, exposed him as only a "gifted young actor."

Moving from the sublime back to the Bs, an anecdote illustrates how one director handled the strain of working with a somewhat handicapped actor while trying to make an acceptable film in eighteen days. James Hogan directed the Drummond series, and knowing the production executives kept a sharp eye on his tussle with time, he devised a clever ploy to keep them off his back. At the end of each day he prepared and rehearsed a big closeup to be shot the next morning. For those unacquainted with filmmaking basics, under ordinary circumstances a big closeup is the easiest set-up to light, and since the camera crew reported on the set at 7:30 A.M., shortly after 9:00, our usual starting time, the big closeup was lit, rehearsed, and shot. However, before saying "cut" Jimmy would approach the mike and announce in a loud clear voice, "First take in the bag, 9:12 A.M." Then, satisfied that the executives would hear the good news when they ran the dailies the following morning, he would settle back, have a fresh cup of coffee, and take a reasonable and relaxed length of time to prepare his next set-up.

From 1932 to 1952 Bs led a pigeonholed existence, but even a film dog will have its day, a day which usually sprouted some new genius. When an A was good it was only achieving its potential, but when a B was, in the local parlance, a sleeper, it not only made news in the film colony, it also paved the way for new careers.

Example: Paramount and Lowe's (MGM's parent company) owned or controlled the greatest number of theaters, and they could afford larger budgets and longer schedules. That meant they averaged a better class of Bs. When a series captured the public fancy, as did Metro's long string of *Andy Hardy* productions, budgets and schedules were often increased to an intermediate B+ level. And the *Andy Hardy*s not only out grossed many of the studio's costlier As, they also spawned a couple of A+ stars.

But the Bs' chief claim to a permanent chapter in the saga of the Golden Age resides in an unexpected field, the field of pure art, although its influence in that sparsely-settled area was not recognized until the '40s, when it surfaced in the work of directors who had successfully negotiated the boggy terrain of the "quickies."

"Edward Dmytryk is the talented young director who is guiding the Kramer Company's *The Juggler* for Columbia release. Dmytryk, stars Kirk Douglas and Milly Vitale and the other principal cast members and crew are filming Michael Blankfort's screen version of his novel in Israel, the locale of the story." 1952.

Many years ago Clifford Odets wrote a rather passionate article complaining that artists in general, and writers in particular, were denied the right to fail. That complaint was nearly as old as art itself, but when applied to filmmaking it had a near-zero validity. At a cost of a dollar's worth of paper, or a piece of canvas and some tubes of paint, artists have always been able to toy with failure. But gambling with millions of dollars borrowed from financiers who expect a return on their investment is a horse of a different color. Whether audiences are fickle or simply perceptive is a moot point, for in either case an art which depends on public approval is by definition a gamble. Whatever his goal, a writer who puts pencil to paper is risking failure, and thousands of inferior films have established that a recording camera will more often stop at three lemons than on the jackpot.

In plain words, Odets was demanding the right to experiment at others' expense, and it might have been interesting, even evolutionary, if some of the '30s' greats had occasionally explored far-out territories. But with a few exceptions they stayed with the sure thing although, as the experienced filmmaker knows, even that does not guarantee success. For its part, the B field was unburdened with high expectations and manned chiefly by veterans who, despite their demonstrated lack of unusual talent, had established their ability to knock out a finished picture under thankless conditions, but it also apprenticed a few beginners who had little to lose and a world to gain. Most of them were seeking fame rather than immediate fortune, since it was safe to assume the second was inevitable if the first was achieved. But they had to get *attention*! And if art was the only way to go, they were willing to give it a try.

The following anecdote (probably apocryphal) has been told before, but it uniquely illustrates the matter of the moment. And that makes it worth repeating.

At the height of his career, C. B. DeMille was dining at the home of Adolph Ochs, the publisher of the New York Times. *They were discussing art, on which subject there was some polite disagreement. After dinner, Ochs led C. B. to his library, stopped as he opened the door, and pointed to a large group painting at the far end of the room.*

"Mr. DeMille, how many people do you see on that canvas?" C. B. studied it through squinted eyes.

"Oh," he said, "perhaps twenty or thirty."

Ochs escorted DeMille to the far end of the room. There, at close range, only three or four people were clearly delineated; the rest were vaguely suggestive blobs of paint.

"That, Mr. DeMille," said Adolph Ochs, "is art."

And it is in that area, where "less is (often) more," that gifted B directors found their deliverance.

In my laudatory treatment of the giants of the '30s, I neglected to mention a widespread weakness: with the exception of Ford, Murnau, and possibly Lubitsch, the great directors—especially the Sennett and Roach graduates—shared a lack of expertise in staging and set-ups.[42] Their early training in slapstick comedies and quickie westerns had placed a premium on full shots and flat lighting, neither of which is conducive to technical brilliance. The set-ups and compositions of Capra, Wyler, Stevens, and McCarey, while adequate, would shame a talented neophyte of today.

If that statement seems to fly in the face of my praise for the '30's top directors it should be understood that technical skills, to reverse a mathematical standard, are neither "necessary nor sufficient" for artistic preeminence in the film world. A well-known Hollywood axiom holds that if viewers leave the theater commenting mainly on the striking photography or the beautiful musical score, the film, as a whole, is a dud. For it is the understanding of substance, of human character, of emotion, motivation, and pace, plus an undefinable instinct for capturing the viewer's heart and mind that is most important. And it is in these areas that the best directors excelled. (Of course, the combination of dramatic substance *and* cinematic technique, as seen in John Ford's work, is unbeatable, as his four Oscars testify.)

Lacking the scripts, the casts, and the schedules of the As, a few ambitious B directors committed themselves to the investigation of those aspects of filmmaking that might command attention without the expenditure of time and money. These were the related arts of staging for the camera point of view (which differs greatly from blocking on the stage), the refinement of set-ups, and the creative use of lighting and lenses.

In the early '40s one of my colleagues, a recruit from Broadway, approached me with "Eureka!" written all over him.

"I've found the secret of staging for the screen!" he enthused. "I just picture a proscenium over all my shots!"

But it is only fair to mention that Rouben Mamoulian and Vincent Minnelli, also from the theater, managed set-ups that were eminently cinematic.

A subdivision of the art of the set-up was the proper employment of foreground pieces, a technique that makes possible a full realization of cinematic art. Based on the principle that the eye measures distance by comparing relative sizes of familiar objects, this practice was (and is) used in conjunction with special lighting to endow an apparent third dimension to a two-dimensional image. A foreground piece, which can be an animate or inanimate object, placed close to the camera, lends a sense of depth to a player in the middle distance. (The effect can be heightened by placing other characters or essential objects at varying distances from the camera.) This was also a long overdue correction of the practice of grouping actors horizontally to enable them to share one microphone, a practice that persisted as an unconscious habit long after the mic was free to travel. (Except in video sitcoms or rare cases of necessity, no knowledgeable film director will line up his actors *across* the screen.) A thorough understanding of the lenses' power to facilitate the evocation of subliminal dramatic effects is also necessary.

Val Lewton was perhaps the only man to make a mark as a producer of Bs. He managed to stand out in this graveyard of talent because of his skill in selecting suspense material in which subject triumphed over dressing, and directors like Jacques Tourneur, Mark Robson, and Robert Wise, who were able to do the material justice. But the early escape of Robson and Wise to major production left Joseph H. (Joe) Lewis as the virtuoso of the Bs. His creative use of foreground pieces in his arresting set-ups, plus the effective offbeat lighting he coaxed out of his cameraman, were envied or admired by every young director (and some of the old). Eventually, as intended, it caught the eye of studio executives, who gave him an A for his efforts. Alas! His talent for imagery failed to divert attention from his lackluster handling of the more essential human aspects of drama, and Joe was soon back in the Bs.

But not for long. He must have been "discovered" a half-dozen times. And though he was hailed as an auteur by French film critics, who generally favored technical ingenuity, he spent most of his long career embellishing inferior substance while setting technical examples for young directors who passed him on their way into the slick and '40s.

Those gifted young filmmakers recognized that technical expertise was largely cosmetic. Their attitude toward their own creations was expressed in the use of words like "tricks," "crotch-shots," and "gruesomes" to describe their more bizarre set-ups. Nevertheless, though clothes don't make the man, they do get other people's attention, and while technical dexterity did not give life to a bad movie, it minimized some of its mistakes and, when used with subtle skill, served to keep the viewer's attention.

The third important contribution to cinematic art was an elaboration (or simplification) of a photographic style. (At this point I feel obliged to admit that none of the foregoing techniques originated with the Bs, but it was in this seedbed that necessity nursed them to full development.) The staging of the scene and the choice of camera set-ups are the total responsibility of the competent director; the lighting of such action and set-ups is the responsibility of the cameraman. But the style or mood of the lighting is, or should be, another element of the director's filmic master plan, although the script's context often makes a choice self-evident.

Throughout the '30s most films were shot in a classic style designed to show the set and its occupants as fully and clearly as possible. However, a twelve-day schedule allowed little time for classic film lighting where even the doorknob gets its own key light, and who wants to settle for half-baked classicism? Well, many did, but the more creative directors worked with the more responsive photographers to perfect a film style that was more striking and effective than conventional lighting, yet required half the time to implement. To oversimplify, it was a version of *chiaroscuro*, or high-contrast lighting, which accentuated the important features of a face or a set while leaving the rest shadowed, indistinct, and a challenge to the viewer's imagination.[43]

Add to this the skillful utilization of staging and set-ups and you've taken a giant step toward a genre that the '40s called "film noir."

(It is appropriate to add that the Bs, which died with the imposition of the consent decree in the early 50s, have reappeared, lock, stock, and barrel on our television sets, both as ongoing series [*Colombo, Perry Mason; Murder, She Wrote*, et al.] and in full-length dramatic features that are too often based on badly distorted "true-life" stories.)

CHAPTER NINETEEN

An old Chinese curse says it all: "May you live in interesting times!"

In such eras anything can happen, and in Hollywood's '40s everything did. The talkies had grown phenomenonally through their first decade, roaring into 1939 like a towering ninth wave. The '40s rode its crest exuberantly until it spattered on the rocks of reaction. Remembered in Hollywood more for their late years of disaster than for their earlier years of fulfillment, the '40s unquestionably comprised the most interesting decade in its history and, coincidentally, in the history of the real world.

While Hollywood was still celebrating the climactic year of 1939, things were happening over which it had no control. Even the community's most eminent crystal-gazers failed to foretell the maelstrom that engulfed the planet when, on the first of September, Hitler's army invaded Poland and Great Britain and France declared war on Germany.

Like a top-rated suspense film it all started very slowly; for the first nine months the face-off created the heat and excitement of a sputtering firecracker and the United States found itself tossed about by colliding currents of opinion. Hollywood, traditionally more liberal than the rest of the country, favored Britain and France, but its policy of neutrality toward any possible patron steered it clear of controversy. Feeling safe, snug, and comfortably isolated between our two vast oceans, Hollywood by and large kept to the middle path.

In May of 1940, Hitler opened the gates of Hell and the world was startled by the abrupt and violent end of the "phony war." The tricky Germans ignored the "impregnable" Maginot Line and swept through

Belgium. In just over two weeks France was finished and Britain's army found itself on occupied soil with nowhere to go but out. It left the Continent in true British style. All available naval ships as well as an armada of private craft skippered by their civilian owners were mobilized to siphon the British Army off the Continent through the Flanders port of Dunkirk. This heroic and successful action swung the tide of opinion in an admiring United States. In Hollywood, Willie Wyler's *Mrs. Mimiver*, celebrating that occasion and the great courage of the British people, swept the Oscars in 1942.

As some philosopher once said, war isn't all bad, especially for the economy of neutral powers and for the rapid development of cosmetic surgery. In the United States Bust turned to Boom as the American embargo on armaments was lifted and factories were called upon to supply materiel for Great Britain and the Soviet Union when, on June 22, 1941, an overconfident Hitler invaded Russia.

Given a positive direction and a growing audience, the studios fell to with renewed vitality. But the involvement became complete when on December 7, 1941, Japanese carrier-based planes wiped out a large part of the American navy in a sneak attack on Pearl Harbor in the Hawaiian Islands. Willy-nilly, the United States was now a fighting ally; isolationism and divided loyalty disappeared. A single emotion, hate, was shared by all and brought us together at last.

Fruit trees bloom profusely when their death is imminent; so do humans. They become euphoric when millions of lives are about to be sacrificed to Mars.[44] Probably because Hollywood was sensitized by the lure of conflict and conditioned to glorify it, its heroes, and its martyrs, war fever hit Hollywood harder and sooner than the public at large. Film workers, artists, stars, and executives, many of whom had opposed the draft, crowded the recruiting stations on the day after Pearl Harbor.

The United States was now the armor of the Free World. Arms factories and munitions plants worked around the clock and exhibitors and film producers profited by cooperating with the war effort, each in his own way.

In most cities theater managers were happy to keep their doors open twenty-four hours a day to help three shifts of factory workers shed the tensions of their toil while they watched films which reminded them whom they were fighting and what they were fighting for. The filmmakers' neverending search for "substance" was now a shoo-in. For the first time since film had grown up there was an ego-subordinating conflict, a conflict in which the United States was a badly-crippled underdog. In films, the combination was hard to beat and easy to dramatize. Germany and Japan had more planes, more tanks, far more men in uniform, and more combat experience; their armies were tempered by battles in Europe and Asia. Although on December 7, 1941, few seasoned gamblers would have bet on the Allies, Hollywood seized the moment and turned it into a field day which lasted many years.

Suddenly, the "message" was in. Germany and Japan were two bullies kicking sand in the face of a handicapped Uncle Sam, and the often-difficult problem of content was replaced by a formula the best Hollywood writers had been trying to forget—white was all white and black was black. There was no need for an exploration of the underlying economic reasons for the war or a cinematic explanation of the enemy's inhuman behavior, which was taken for granted.

In the early '40s, however, war films were by no means the totality of Hollywood's output, and most of those made were the equivalent of B action pictures promoted to A category by star power and A production schedules. Story costs were minimal; after substituting despot-worshiping Germans and Japanese for outlaws, horse-thieves, and Indians, the old plotlines still filled the bill.

Except for an interesting modification.

Filmmakers soon learned that propaganda was a rather special field. We were no longer dealing with quasi-mythical figures like Earp or Jesse James; we were trying to rationalize reality. It was not easy to convince an extremely non-homogenous population, much of which shared ancestry with the enemy, that the stock from which they came was inherently less humane than they were. There seemed to be little doubt that our viewers both in and out of the military, needed to be convinced that somehow the enemy soldier, or even their man-in-the-street, deserved no better treatment than a contagion-carrying mosquito or a plant-devouring gopher. Perhaps the most effective strategy was to place the blame on individuals, on Hitler, Hirohito, and even the comic Mussolini; but it was impossible to explore these characters in depth. No one could explain how and why so many previously sane men and women could approve of the cruelties and butcheries of their half-mad leaders, so no one tried. It was enough to dramatize the results of their evil attitudes and their merciless actions.

Bs were made to order for the attack on the Axis; the first of these were peopled by German spies and/or infiltrators. But romantic novels had made such characters more glamorous than threatening and a more direct kind of propaganda was called for. For instance, *Hitler's Children*, made at RKO, was based on what was known of the Fuhrer's work battalions and his drive to breed an Aryan race, but a budget of $100,000 hardly created visions of crowded theaters. However, miracles do happen, and *Hitler's Children* was such a huge success that it was largely credited with pulling the studio out of the red. It was also my passport into the Big Time. But before it came out I was asked to make another B propaganda film, *Behind the Rising Sun*. Like *Hitler's Children*, it was laid in an enemy country and dealt with that country's people.

The propaganda was not in the basic plot, which could have been as easily made in Japan about an American family, but in the background material based largely on newspaper accounts of the earlier Sino-Japanese war as seen by Western journalists. (Much of the enemy's brutality incorporated in the film was later verified by Japanese army footage which became available after Japan's surrender.)

Such films created an interesting side effect. Argentina was allied with the Axis and the West's propaganda films were forbidden in that country. However, they were widely known, the want-to-see factor was high, and ingenious Uruguayan exhibitors took advantage of the boycott. Argentineans could (and did) buy tickets which included passage on the night-boat across the Rio de la Plata estuary to Uruguay, a showing of the banned films in a theater in Montevideo, and a boat trip back to Buenos Aires.

Hating to see all that money go across the river, Argentine exhibitors clipped a sequence from Behind the Rising Sun *which featured a fight between an American boxer (played by Robert Ryan) and a Japanese jiu-jitsu expert (played by Mike Mazurki) and ran it, uncredited, to SRO crowds in their theaters.*

During the Great Depression people with means had been encouraged to rescue the economy by squandering a little more than they could judiciously afford. Now there were jobs in plenty and money to spend, but little to spend it on. Although visitors from Great Britain might consider our rationing a bit of a joke, few Americans were laughing. The automobile plants were building jeeps, personnel carriers, tanks, and land-

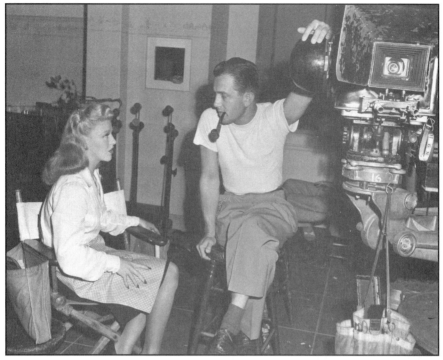

Eddie Dmytryk directing Ginger Rogers in *Tender Comrade*, 1943.

ing craft instead of family sedans, the rubber plantations were largely in Japanese hands, new tires were nowhere to be found, and gasoline was strictly rationed. Women's skirts were shortened, cuffs deleted from men's pants, and even "Lucky Strike green had gone to war!"[45]

However, America's reservoir of gun fodder was so huge that only a small percentage of its manpower was actually in harm's way; the majority of Americans were feeling only the slight sting of shortages and hate alone was not enough to fuel the sacrificial home fires. Something more was needed to keep the factory workers' noses to their grindstones, especially since that old saw had acquired a broader meaning—many of the noses now belonged to women. To sustain a healthy morale at home it was essential to recognize that Rosie the Riveter was as worthy of support as the G. I. Joe in North Africa or on Guadalcanal. Propaganda to awaken such appreciation was vital, and once more Hollywood answered the call.

The spate of war pictures—*Thirty Seconds Over Tokyo, Dive Bomber, A Guy Named Joe*, et al.—were now augmented by the adventures of those who worked and waited at home. My first A film, *Tender Comrade*, joined *Mrs. Miniver, Since You Went Away, So Proudly We Hail*, and a score of others in dramatizing the lonely but busy lives of those who filled in for their men while awaiting their return. *Tender Comrade*, starring Ginger Rogers, told the story of four women who get together to share companionship and expenses while laboring in the war effort. (Four years later their motto, "Share and share alike," got me into serious trouble with the Committee on Un-American Activities and played havoc with my career.)

Almost without exception such films were excessively sentimental—today they seem embarrassingly maudlin—but those were times of stress and people overdosed on love.

The home-front films did well at the box office, not always because of their content but because of their "names." The war had sidetracked only some of the stars, for, believe it or not, in the '30s and '40s women were as bankable as men. Katherine Hepburn, Irene Dunne, Olivia DeHaviland, Ginger Rogers, Norma Shearer, Joan Crawford, Claudette Colbert, Jennifer Jones, Ingrid Bergman, Bette Davis, Rosalind Russell, Mae West, Marlene Dietrich, and, of course, the great Garbo shone as brightly as any male star. As a matter of fact, most of the male stars broke in as supporting leads for actresses: Cary Grant for Mae West and Rosalind Russell, Fred MacMurray for Claudette Colbert, Joel McCrea for several leading women, Paul Henreid and a host of males for Bette Davis. Even the "king" played second fiddle to Joan Crawford at the start of his reign. The list is long and the reason is not hard to find.

Love stories!

Great romances like *Camille* and *Wuthering Heights* were staples of the '30s, but the early '40s especially needed a strong antidote for the hate and violence being peddled on a global scale, and the love story remained the *pièce de resistance* of the motion-picture palaces. Although many, as usual, were based on trite soldier-meets-girl themes, some of the films—*Random Harvest* and *Waterloo Bridge*, for instance—are still classic romances.[46] And in romances, women carry the load. Today, with peep-show sex and excessive violence as the *plat du jour*, women, with rare exceptions, are of secondary importance.

It is significant of Hollywood's artistic health in the early '40s that six of 1944's Ten Best Films had nothing to do with the war. They were *Going My Way, Gaslight, The Song Of Bernadette, Madame Curie, Dragon Seed*, and *The Story Of Dr. Wassel*. Four of these starred women at the top, indicating that the creative momentum of the '30s had not been derailed by the war—at least not by the "hot" war.

The sharp-eyed film buff will notice that *Going My Way* (1944) was the first musical, or rather, story with music, to win the Oscar since *The Great Ziegfeld* in 1936. It also won a second Oscar for its director, Leo McCarey, and a first for crooner Bing Crosby, for Best Performance. Although musicals were rarely considered "heavy" enough for Academy honors, the burgeoning popularity of pop music on the radios and the movie screens of the 30s transplanted nearly the total population of Tin Pan Alley to Hollywood and filled its melody cup to overflowing.

Films like *The Gold Diggers* (1933) and *42nd Street* (1933) from Warner Brothers paved the way for MGM's *The Great Ziegfeld* (1935), RKO's Astaire and Rogers series, and the sequential releases of *Paramount On Parade* and MGM's *Broadway Melody*. And it was not surprising that by the start of World War II the studios found audiences were harmonically sated.

However, after a few years a war-weary public needed an antidote for its long and heavily-felt presence, and by the early '40s it was ready for a resurgence of music and dancing. "Watercades" like *Bathing Beauty* (1944) and straight musicals like *Anchors Aweigh* and a new MGM series of Astaire features restored the musical to a position of prominence for a number of years.

As the war drew slowly to a close, film distributors, like ancient camp followers, tagged after the Allied armies in their reclamation of occupied territories. The pickings were rich, but though American music was popular, the same could not be said for Yankee lyrics which were nearly impossible to dub into foreign languages. From then on, with few exceptions, the only musicals produced were those which promised a profit in English-speaking areas alone.

However, the Pandora's box which poured its contents onto the studios in the late '40s made the musical's problems hardly worth the pity.

CHAPTER TWENTY

A new wave of talented immigrants rolled into Hollywood in the late '30s and early '40s, replenishing the studios' pool of original thinkers and contributing to the body and the soul of the film community. This second surge of European talent was headed by established film artists of all categories who had waited until the last moment in the hope that Hitler was a temporary phenomenon. They were more diverse than the immigrants of the earlier '30s, and their reasons for coming to California were based less on Hollywood's superior technology or its get-rich-quick potential than on a desire to take advantage of that which, until recently, was noticed only in its absence—the freedom of artistic thought and expression. Nearly all were liberal, and most were convinced the film medium was vital to society's reconstruction if, or when, fascism was defeated.

In the meantime the realization that the movies now reached an audience far greater than that of any other art form proved a catalyst to a younger theater generation in our own country, and the small stream of old-world intellectuals was joined by a torrent of invaders from Broadway. "Heading for Hollywood" (which is not the same as "going Hollywood") was no longer considered a backward step but an opportunity. The theater still offered respect but the flicks offered a far greater congregation whose acceptance approached worship.

The influx of new blood, however, had little immediate influence on a Hollywood luxuriating in its heyday. Films were now big business, and the bigger the business the smaller the disposition for change. Concepts and techniques which had once been new became rigid rules, and free-ranging experimentation had given way to size and slickness. In A films, all-star casts were the rule and to show them at their best photography achieved new highs in clarity and gloss if not in mood and subtlety. The world market and drive-in theaters were responsible for much of this development, since only a bright, unambiguous picture could pass muster outdoors or when subjected to the dated and dim projection systems in the less-developed corners of the world.

But development resists complacency, and inevitably, the technical language needed to facilitate the investigation of new frontiers grew to applicable proportions. Orson Welles, a natural-born rule-breaker, borrowed his camera techniques from others (especially John Ford and Friedrich Murnau), but he deserves sole credit for liberating the picture from the lingering grip of the sound engineers by a greatly increased use of looping, or post-synching, of dialogue. This technique did much to broaden the field of effective set-ups by allowing the director to eliminate the microphone and its boom when lighting demands made such a move advisable.

Although *Citizen Kane* was savaged by personal press attacks and failed at the box office, its positive aspects far outweighed its negative viewer reception, especially with the younger filmmakers, and prodded Hollywood into a short extension of the Golden Age. An aura of new creativity pervaded the town. Perhaps the most striking advances of the period were in the areas of class and character and in the development of film noir, which gained status as the fussy, over fastidious strictures placed on attitudes and appearance began to lose their force (though not without a fight).

As mentioned earlier, intimations of film noir appeared occasionally in the B films of the '30s and in a few segments as far back as the silents, but their appearances were too random and disjunctive to be recognized as the building blocks of a breakaway style. Eventually the compatibility of the "lower depths" of our society and their interpretation through chiaroscuro lighting and subliminally distorting lenses was recognized by the more creative directors. But it was only when those indefatigable analysts, the French critics and students of the cinema, created a pigeonhole marked Film Noir that the style was legitimized with a name and a seat at the Captain's table. Several films had already been made in Hollywood that fit the new genre, and none illustrates it better than *Murder, My Sweet*, since it was that film which brought about a perfect union of story and style with the writing of the idiosyncratic Raymond Chandler and the techniques of film noir.

Murder, My Sweet (1944) created some stir at the box office and with the critics. Shortly after its release I ran into Mervyn LeRoy, one of MGM's top filmmakers. He had recently seen the film and he patted my shoulder in a senior-statesmanlike gesture of friendliness.

"I enjoyed your film very much," he said. "But why did you make it so dark?"

I mumbled something about pertinent mood photography. That was long before I first heard the term film noir, and I was thinking of his own dark period with films like Little Caesar *and* I Am A Fugitive From A Chain Gang. *Still, that was more than a dozen years ago, and people do change…*

Of course, there were 'who-done-its' long before *Murder, My Sweet*. Germany's *M*, for instance, was a film which might have been seen as film noir if that classification had been postulated a few years earlier. But they were a comparative trickle until Chandler's spotlighting of the mean streets of L.A. and its environs widened a crack in the dike that no human finger could plug. The phrase excited the fancies of students of the genre everywhere and started a spate of film noir that ruled the screens of the country for over two decades.

The "mean streets" of L.A. soon became a metaphor for the mean streets of the world. In Hollywood it was a signal, though largely ignored as such, that hundreds of years of American Puritanism was nearing an end. The phrase was an "open sesame" that exposed a cave-full of material for the dramatization of evil, which has always been more exciting, more interesting, and more entertaining than good, and for many years writers and directors scoured every alley and rummaged through every dumpster in their search for film noir material. Then, like a replay of the Mongols' self-destructive conquest of China, the essence of film noir was diluted by assimilation. Today, few good films are made without the use of chiaroscuro lighting, wide angle lenses, and offbeat set-ups, the technical trademarks of the genre. As for the incorporation of netherworld characters and the preoccupation with evil, in the '90s even movies for children exploit the field.

But the exposure of the dark side of our society was not necessarily a mirror; it could also be an interpretation. The easing of strictures, which had opened the way to the exploitation of murder and mayhem, encouraged some of the more concerned filmmakers (and there are always a few) to take advantage of the enhanced techniques and the studios' increased indulgence in a campaign against some of the real evils of society, those evils of which mayhem and murder are only the surface signs. Bigotry, class hatred, xenophobia, and social prejudice in general had been largely left untouched by the older filmmakers, who tacitly agreed such social

When artistic black and white lighting set the mood calling for little dialogue. Edward Dmytryk's *Crossfire*. 1947, RKO. Robert Ryan and Robert Young at right of picture.

conflicts were neither tasteful nor profitable. Although the country's very makeup confronted its citizens with these problems, they were kept under cover by the generally accepted myth of the melting pot, a concept of which all Americans, ignoring its contradictions, were very proud.

However, our propaganda attacks against the moral transgressions of our enemies had opened a can of worms and, buoyed up by our victory over the Axis, a few of Hollywood's younger filmmakers, who were aware that friend and foe were not all that different, decided the time was ripe for a public examination of some of our own less-attractive attitudes.

Fortunately *The Brick Foxhole*, a murder drama against a backdrop of social awareness written by Richard Brooks, was available, and the price was ridiculously low since the very qualities which made it good reading

Low-key lighting was the important element in helping actor Robert Ryan to portray the bad guy in *Crossfire*. Most important!

also made it a poor bet in the film market. More to the point, it appeared to have an unbeatable problem. The novel, in part, involved a random hate killing of a homosexual; the murder was unobjectionable to the censor but the mention of that word or visualization of the character murdered was taboo under the Code. Absolutely!

So the victim became a Jew, which was just fine with the censors, and the hunt for a motive that, in this case, did not involve the customary considerations of familiarity, personal acquaintance, kinship, theft, jealousy, or greed was the story's spine.

The resulting film, made in 1947 and entitled *Crossfire*, was the first motion picture to deal with a major ethnic prejudice, and the studio's hesitation in releasing it created a suspense almost as great as that in the film. But after numerous previews before various social and religious groups (all very positive), the film was released.

The critics raved,[47] the box office returns were very strong, and a random poll indicated that a significant number of prejudiced viewers had been moved to re-examine their biases. And that took me back a few months.

After my post-production showing for the composer and the sound effects crew a young Argentinean from the music department caught up with me on the steps of the commissary.

"Mr. Dmytryk," he said, "I just want to tell you how much I enjoyed the film. But why did you include that stuff about anti-Semitism?"

I was taken aback. "That was our chief reason for making the picture," I said.

"But there's no anti-Semitism in the United States," he protested. "If there were, why is all the money in America controlled by Jewish bankers?"

Oh, well, I thought, you can't win 'em all. I went in and had lunch.

That should have been a warning. But Elia Kazan's *Gentleman's Agreement* followed hot on the heels of *Crossfire*, and was also well-received by the critics, the public, and Hollywood. At last it seemed the dream of taking innumerable steps "into another world of thinking and doing" was suddenly realizable. A few of us began to chart the road into that promised land and its untapped wealth of material. But we had forgotten to touch wood, which has nothing to do with superstition and everything to do with reality; it is a reminder that the pendulum must reverse its swing, that progress is a cyclical process, and that one must look in both directions before crossing the street.

Note—RKO considered a film dealing with anti-Semitism a very high risk, so Adrian Scott, the producer, and I agreed to make it for $500,000. We assembled an expensive cast, which gave us little money for production and a near-B schedule of twenty-two days. But research had disclosed that an average A film at RKO spent eighty percent of its time on preparation and lighting and only twenty percent on rehearsal and shooting. I asked Roy Hunt, one of Hollywood's best and most cooperative cinematographers, if he could turn those figures around. He knew I wanted a film noir look and he agreed without a moment's hesitation. I helped by simplifying my set-ups, and Hunt and I managed to get the look and performances of an eighty-day film in twenty days.

CHAPTER TWENTY-ONE

It was summer of 1945. The war was over, disclosing a problem that had lain dormant for the duration: what was to be done with the huge inventory of wet goods not wasted in the war? Millions of young men were coming home and the results of their long-dreamed-of separation from the service were not always pleasant. Many of the 'liberated' were dangling in the wind, feeling less like honorably-discharged heroes than like paroled prisoners. They, too, had lived elbow-to-elbow with violence and death, and now the streets of a nonbelligerent society were an unfamiliar and sometimes frightening wilderness. If they were not a totally "lost" generation, they were certainly one that had been left behind. But they would soon have company.

A growing awareness of the problems suffered by returning soldiers did little to identify the stateside war anxieties, apprehensions that had affected many of those who had kept the home fires burning, qualms that had been conveniently buried during the war and the euphoria that immediately followed. However, reality returned almost immediately as our former ally, now the world's other super-power, became the Evil Empire and, unrecognized by most battle-weary citizens, the Cold War was under way. Cataclysmic changes, made worse by the global convulsions of World War II, now asserted themselves, and the second half of the century's fifth decade was a potpourri of progress and regression, of hope and fear, of love and acrimonious hate.

Hollywood, which mirrors more often than it interprets or inspires, changed as the world changed and, as was true of the world as a whole, not in a positive direction. Although the younger generation of filmmakers had opened their minds to new possibilities and broader ideas, both foreign and domestic, and were ready to show a world according to newer gospels, they were naively unaware that older hands wanted nothing more than a return to the good old days. Even now they were scheming how to get back there.

For those willing to look into the future there were ominous clouds on the horizon. Early in 1947 Peter Rathvon, RKO's top executive, dolefully pointed out to a group of studio producers and directors that while peace was a blessing for the world it was a setback for the film industry. Revenues were falling as factories abandoned night shifts and theaters no longer enjoyed the financial windfalls of twenty-four-hours-a-day showings to customers who were spending their wages on products the war had long denied them. That alone would hardly have put the quietus on a healthy golden age but it was only the beginning. More—much more—was waiting in the wings.

Almost immediately three major crises, all seeded in earlier times, surfaced and brought an unexpected end to Hollywood's renaissance, changing its course, its makeup, and, most traumatically, the quality of its product. It all started late in 1947, when a Congressional committee determined to expose what they and some jittery Hollywood personalities believed was a pack of dangerous Hollywood leftists. The second crisis involved the judicial branch of the government when, in May of 1948, the Supreme Court of the United States issued its consent decree. The third crisis was little noticed by studio executives even when, in 1949, statistics showed that one million television sets were siphoning off an audience that had once been the exclusive property of film.

Creativity is by no means limited to the artistic world, but there is one glaring characteristic which sets off the working artists from their fellow men and women: they are compelled to express their opinions (and, incidentally, themselves) whether in words or in works, to as much of the world as they can successfully attract. It is vital to their well-being that others see and hear what they have to show and tell, and until they accomplish that goal to some measurable extent, they are not counted as artists, and certainly not as successes.

In keeping with this compulsion it is natural for most artists to feel a special attachment to the Constitution's First Amendment, which guarantees freedom of speech and, inferentially, freedom of thought. And though artists are as human as the next person, and often challenge each other's words and concepts, whether philosophical or political, they reach near-

Edward Dmytryk.

unanimity in their support of the right to free expression for all if only because objection to such a freedom might endanger their own.

Yet it was a challenge to this concept of freedom that was most responsible for bringing an end to Hollywood's Golden Age. Spurred on by the sharp political divisions engendered by the Cold War, Hollywood spawned a movement to sanctify the old and stifle the new which, in the language of politics, meant the elimination of Socialism and especially its dangerous relative, Communism.

In self-defense a number of aging film people formed a group that, apparently unaware of the irony, they called "The Motion Picture Alliance for the Preservation of American Ideals." At its urging, on October 27, 1947 (another "date in infamy"), the House Committee on Un-American Activities opened hearings to investigate the need, even the obligation, to curtail the Constitutional rights of anyone whose views might carry a pink or reddish tinge.

The inquisition that followed was the hottest news of the year; it was widely reported by the American media and by the world press, and nearly half a century later its subdued echoes still linger.[48] However, few at the time realized that the sun was setting on Hollywood's Golden Age except for those European intellectuals who recognized the symptoms and, abandoning their American citizenships, hurried back to their home countries, leaving behind a poorer culture that has not yet been restored. Just as the suppression of free thought, particularized by the execution of Socrates, brought an end to the short but brilliant Golden Age of Periclean Athens, so the Congressional hearings into all aspects of the entertainment world, and its prosecution and jailing of the Hollywood Ten, effectively choked creativity in Hollywood as fear of reactionary retribution dogged every producer, writer, and director in town, and made "cowards of [them] all."

The blacklists and the extensive and more frightening "gray" lists that inevitably followed threatened every studio employee, from the laborer behind his coffee-urn on the set to the president in his commodious office. One estimate states that at least two thousand artisans and artists lost their careers in the witch hunts that continued for at least twenty years, and whose crippling side effects have extended to the second and third generations. Beyond any argument the extremists of the right came closer to delivering a death-blow to the filmmakers' search for truth as they saw it than did anything or anyone else in Hollywood's long history. As if that weren't enough, two coincident crises conspired to change the nature of the film market and destroy the world's grand movie palaces as well as the remarkable studio system which had carried films through the Golden Age.

Fate was now on a roll and within six months of the official establishment of the blacklists it delivered its second blow. After years of wrangling between the country's independent exhibitors and the major studio distributors, the Supreme Court of the United States issued a so-called "consent decree," which curtailed the industry's monopolistic practices. It ordered the five major studios to divest themselves of the means of exhibiting their motion pictures.

For decades the majors had been building, buying, or leasing chains of film houses and palaces which assured prime running time for their own films. First-run capability had allowed them to skim the cream off the top of the market, and a very rich cream it was. To maintain their advantage they had invested far more money in theater properties and operations than in their means of production. These huge operations,

The party gets wilder. Photo never before seen! Eddie Dmytryk going after the King, Clark Gable, who seems to be enjoying it all. *Soldier of Fortune* (Hong Kong location), 1955.

which also involved worldwide distribution and exhibition, mandated parent-company offices in New York that employed personnel largely unknown to the men and women in Hollywood who made the product which was the foundation of the entire industry.

The average filmmaker, on a film's completion, watched his picture disappear into the maw of the home office in New York, usually with relief, since most film artists had little taste for commerce. Yet New York was the center where releases and release dates were arranged, where promotion, advertising, and selling took place—in short, the business that ensured a picture's profit and, incidentally, gave the filmmaker the means to make further works of art and enjoy a good living.

By the early '50s the consent decree was in full operation; each studio's distribution department had to auction its films to the highest bidders, and practice a sometimes reluctant detachment in awarding opening dates. All of this was an inconvenience, of course, but more troublesome was the fact that cash flow channels had been designed (probably for tax purposes) to allot a greater share of a film's earnings to distribution than to production. (I was surprised to learn at Rathvon's cost lecture that a production facility often showed a paper loss which was more than covered by the overall profits of the parent company.) Now the studios, divested of their theaters, had to demand

EDWARD
DMYTRYK
DIRECTOR

THE
CAINE MUTINY

Color by Technicolor • A COLUMBIA PICTURE

Dmytryk's Golden Age.

a larger slice of the pie if they were to survive. This led to a juggling of financial formulae which did not achieve stability for a number of years.

One morning the Hollywood press reported that Marlon Brando's deal for making One-Eyed Jacks, *which was soon to start shooting, would give him ninety percent of the profits. I was flabbergasted and still a bit shell-shocked when I ran into Y. Frank Freeman, Paramount's studio head, in the commissary.*

"Frank," I almost shouted, "how can you give Brando ninety percent of the profits? You're giving him the picture!"

Freeman smiled. "Oh," he said, "we would have given him a hundred if he had insisted. Because we know something he doesn't. There aren't going to be any profits.*"*

Any CPA who knows a little about the complex bookkeeping employed in the film business can explain that one. And so can a number of actors and directors who are still waiting for their share of the grosses of films which were undeniably box office hits.

Years earlier I had received a call from William Dieterle, who was looking for help. He had just seen the morning trade papers, and he was in a quandary.

"Eddie," he wailed. "I have just read that Salome has so far earned nine million dollars, and it only cost two. How can I get my cut of the picture?"

"Sue the studio," I advised. "That is, if you don't want to work here any longer."

Sinatra understood the system better than most. "Get it up front," he said.

The third crisis was the *coup de grâce*; final, inevitable, but delivered in slow motion. It was disguised as progress, and naturally it was obstinately unacknowledged at first. Then, when its existence could no longer be ignored, it was fought to a bitter end. Quite simply, the "problem" was that the 17,000 TV sets found in American households in 1947 had exploded to 32,000,000 by 1954. And that was only the beginning.

It was 1955, and we had stopped off in Tokyo while on our way to Hong Kong to shoot Soldier Of Fortune, *starring Clark Gable. A press conference was obligatory, and a sizable meeting hall was crammed with at least a hundred members of the press. Gable and I sat at a table facing the crowd. The first question had just been asked and translated when Gable suddenly rose to his feet. He had noticed something that had escaped my attention. At the back of the room several TV cameras had been set up to record the interview, and Gable pointed a finger in that direction.*

"I will not respond to any question until those cameras have been removed from this room," he said, in his firmest tone. "Those are my enemies!"

There was a brief flurry at the rear of the hall, then, accompanied by puzzled but polite murmuring from the assembled reporters, the cameras were quickly trundled away. When the door closed on "the enemy," Gable sat down.

"Now—what was the question?" he asked.

That was already too late in the day. For many years the leaders of the motion picture industry had ignored the growth of "the enemy," a medium even more revolutionary than their own had been. Whether, like their presumptuous talkies, this was a healthy addition to the field of entertainment remained to be seen, but it certainly could not be halted by willful denial. By the time their eyes were fully opened, most of the advantages they might have enjoyed because of their established primacy in the entertainment media were firmly in the networks' hands. The eventual result was compromise. The major studios were forced to join the brash newcomer and, unfortunately, compete with TV on its level, a level which, by common consent, has not approached the quality of the films of the golden years.

Chapter Twenty-two

In the ring three knockdowns in a single round brings a fight to an abrupt finish, but not in the film capital. In spite of being lambasted high and low by Congress, by the Supreme Court, and by Television, Hollywood, while bloodied and on its knees, has managed to survive the TKO. And though its standards are lower it continues to supply the world's theaters with its product while shaking the cobwebs out of its collective head and shaking some heads out with the cobwebs. Some observers, however, believe that the ringing in Hollywood's ears will never disappear.

Making comparisons is a ticklish operation, especially for an old-timer. Ordinarily the boast "We did it better in the old days," is difficult to support. However, in this case a defense need not be called upon; a number of classics networks have given both old and young the opportunity to make comparisons not based on nostalgia, and their generally-accepted designation of Hollywood's super-productive years as The Golden Age of Filmmaking precludes any debate.

Nevertheless, we must play fair. Golden Ages are known by and for their best work; no one records the names or efforts of the mercifully forgotten hacks of the day, but finding films of any period worth remembering is made easy by their height above the surrounding sea of mediocrity and just plain shoddy work. This is especially true of filmmaking today which, as the most glamorous of the arts, attracts hosts of men and women of unreliable talent. It was also true of the Golden Age, but to a lesser extent.

Those bright days were also inundated with films which ranged from the mediocre to the painful, yet on the average the good were notably

Jean and Eddie Dmytryk, 1999.

Edward's STAR on Hollywood Walk of Fame
(Hollywood Boulevard in front of Pantages Theater).

better and somewhat more numerous than they are now, and the bad were not as noxious and certainly not as obscene. Perhaps a quote from Anthony Lane says it (nearly) all. In his review of a current film in *The New Yorker* of June 13, 1994, he writes: "…[it] is the kind of thing that Hollywood does best right now, although that's not saying much; it's the only thing that Hollywood can do…nobody makes musicals, or epics, and the comedies are no laughing matter." And Kenneth Turan, in the *Los Angeles Times* on June 7, 1996, has this to say about a budding box office champion: "A picture that believes that bigger and louder is better, that success goes to whatever makes the most noise and does the most damage…epitomizes trends in Hollywood filmmakers that have made many people rich while impoverishing audiences around the world."

Of course Mr. Lane and Mr. Turan would probably admit Hollywood slips up now and then, making an occasional epic even today. Once in a while a *Dead Poets Society*, a *Philadelphia*, or a *Schindler's List* rises like an Everest above the others. And here there are contradictions and indications. In the opinion of many, Spielberg crashed into film's Valhalla not because of his many profitable and entertaining special-effects films which have made him the period's biggest moneymaker, but with *Schindler's List*, which deals with both a bad and a good aberration of the human spirit. In this regard, one of his friends noted, "Spielberg has found his soul."

As for the average viewing of today, it can only be said in the filmmakers' defense that they do, perhaps, fulfill their purpose by mirroring, or catering to, a sick society. In 1983 Norman Cousins wrote: "We are turning out young men and women who are superbly trained but poorly educated. They are a how-to generation, less concerned with the nature of things than with the working of things. They are beautifully skilled but intellectually underdeveloped. They know everything that is to be known about the functional requirements of their trade but very little about the *human situation* that serves as the context for their work."[49]

And that, though brief, is an analysis in-depth that currently applies to all the arts. Technical expertise, or special effects, has replaced context, which is not as easily communicated or understood. Perhaps another very old sci-fi prophecy is finally being realized: artificial stimulation of the senses is here! Instead of a tug at the heart or a gentle nudging of the mind, the viewer now gets a shock, a "shot in the arm," whether it is a victim ejected from a forty-story window, a car flying off a cliff, a gallon of blood on the carpet, a boat exploding into an all-consuming fire, or a peep-show version of an all-consuming "love."

But the problems that beset our society during film's golden years which, treated dramatically or comedically, were grist for the filmmaker's mill, have not disappeared. Some have been ameliorated, but poverty, ignorance, racism, and what appears to be a world drive for an impossible "ethnic purity" are still with us. And none of the pious pontification extant can possibly achieve a political or religious reconstruction of the 19th-century family in a 21st-century society. Which leaves the resuscitation of our moral and ethical standards a nearly impossible undertaking.

It has been suggested, though certainly not by the teachers, that schools assume that responsibility, but the ever-increasing number of children in an overpopulated world makes it difficult if not impossible to teach even the three Rs.

However, the field is wide open for the one medium which has the money, the time, the equipment already in place, and the means for finding the talent for the job, if it only cares to use it. Although the overwhelming number of films made in the last three decades can hardly be said to have had a positive influence on anyone—young or old—there are still many people of good taste, high standards, and great ability, even in Hollywood, and the market has been known to react to the pendulum's swing. In other words, though little is left to bring joy to the world's "huddled masses," there is still hope.

NOTES

1. Candy was not allowed inside the theater, neither were drinks or popcorn—possession could bring instant expulsion. In those days the exhibitors profited from the films they showed, not from the candy they sold.

2. See Sarah Bernhardt in *Queen Elizabeth*.

3. Much of what is said about comedy holds true for drama. It all depends on the "spin."

4. A recent documentary from England would indicate that Chaplin's method was inspired revision of frequent error.

5. This style of shooting was later used as a time-saving technique by B directors faced with the restrictions of an inadequate schedule. It was called 'doing a Lou King,' after Louis King, Henry's younger brother. Lou was given the unwarranted credit for inventing a technique that eliminated extra lighting time by switching to a narrower lens without changing the set-up, or moving the camera straight into a close-up without changing the lens. Either method 'stole' a second set-up without the necessity of relighting it.

6. The title, 'film editor,' was rarely heard in Hollywood during the silent era. Fancy names for various film crafts arrived shortly after the formation of the Guilds in the mid-30s.

7. 'Trims' are the unused portions of scenes that have been cut into the edited film. The total footage of the trims in any production greatly exceeds the footage used in the finished film.

8. Editing by computer, without any actual cutting involved, has made all its predecessors obsolete.

9. "Undercranking' is probably a confusing term to the non-professional. Simply stated, it means operating the camera at less than standard speed. The slower the camera runs the faster the action as seen on the screen. The effect is best demonstrated in an exaggerated form in Mack Sennett's comedies.

10. Before electric motors were available, camera cranking speed was at the mercy of the camera operator. 60 f/p/m was the ideal, but it depended completely on the operator's sense of timing.

11. In carrying out this concept I often found it additionally advantageous, when problems of dialogue or music pitch were not involved, to undercrank two or three frames a second.

12. There is no way to determine when a film was made on the basis of dates cited in film encyclopedias. The given dates are usually the dates of the films' releases. But the production probably occurred many months, a year, or especially in cases of foreign films, several years previously.

13. It is possible that *Variety* and especially *Sunrise* were seen in their original versions on their first releases. It is impossible to learn when the films were mangled. But such arbitrary editing by distributors and exhibitors has always been with us. The organizations that own the films think nothing of trashing even those which have been acknowledged as art, whether it be by hapless editing or colorization.

14. The seeming contradiction is not the result of the technical quality of present-day sound, which greatly surpasses earlier standards, but of Stanley Kowalski acting techniques and the too-heavy layered use of sound effects and music.

15. *The Liveliest Art*—Arthur Knight—MacMillan Pub. Co. New York, N.Y.

16. Movietone was the trade name for a system which recorded both sound and picture on the same strip of 35mm film.

17. After two or three years of strangely stubborn resistance, Warners surrendered to Westrex sound on film.

18. When such films were played in the United States, some titles in English were customarily added, on the grounds, I assumed, that what was perfectly clear to an illiterate *muzhik* was not easily understood by the average American.

19. The blimp was a heavy sound-proofed metal "overcoat" which enveloped each individual camera and muffled its sound.

20. Millennia of theatrical conditioning and the temptation to show off are hard to suppress, and after more than sixty years of talkies some of these practices, though greatly diminished, still survive.

21. What goes on inside an actor as he takes on a new character with unfamiliar characteristics is another matter, one in which the director is often deeply involved.

22. Sometime during the '50s Peal and Sons, boot makers to George V of England and arguably the best cobblers in the world, mailed out a sad letter. They would continue to repair the shoes they had previously made, they wrote, but they could accept no orders for new ones. The reason? They were short-handed—young people were no longer willing to learn the shoemaker's art.

23. In those glory days men and women who resembled the actors as much as possible were chosen as stand-ins.

24. None of the above-mentioned categories, or "pools," now exist. Today any actor of prominence is a free agent, and that has brought more problems than profit to the industry.

25. In this context synching means matching the words to lip movements already filmed. To replace American dialogue successfully with, say, Chinese or Finnish words is difficult even today—imagine 1929.

26. Much of the inadequate cutting often seen in films, and especially in video, is due to the editors' inability to recognize, or deal with, the ramifications of their craft. Fortunately for them, film editing is such an esoteric art that few people, in or out of the studios, can identify bad cutting. Unfortunately for the viewer, "good-enough" editing almost always diminishes the quality of the film, whether or not it is recognized as a weak link in the production. On the other hand, fine cutting is noticed only by the experts.

27. Both monitored and open previews have affirmed that a silent scene of action (not necessarily violent) still holds the viewer's attention more closely and viscerally than the best of dialogue scenes.

28. McCarey won Oscars for directing *The Awful Truth* (1937) and *Going My Way* (1944). Both films were situation comedies.

29. Leo had a habit of turning to look at his crew's reactions after completing a good take. One large electrician always greeted his enquiring gaze with a slow, dead-pan wink. "I had to get rid of him," said McCarey. "I thought he was on to me."

30. A cut made at the proper picture frame deleted nineteen or more frames of accompanying sound. on the other hand, a cut delayed to accommodate the sound added nineteen or more frames of superfluous picture. And overlapping sound, a commonly-used device, was impossible. The real editing was done during the cutting of the negative, when sound and picture finally occupied separate strips of film.

31. Some time later I found out that his purpose was not to impress the Americans but to be able to return to the "old country" and report that he had worked at the Paramount Studios in the States. He assured me a job would be a twenty-four carat certainty.

32. Some writers still speak in terms of acts. In doing so they subconsciously limit their freedom of scope.

33. I always warned my cast and crew that after forty days the onset of paranoia was a strong possibility, and an awareness of that condition would help to keep it under wraps.

34. What is implied in these words may seem illogical but, as they work, the good directors keep some part of their minds always open for the odd creative slant or any new concept that may pop up at any time, not only for the scene being shot but for scenes down the road. The accommodation of such brainstorms can sometimes wreak havoc with the most careful planning.

35. I heard this dictum from one of Hollywood's top executives as late as 1953.

36. In fairness it must be mentioned that the cessation of censorship allowed filmmakers to tackle a greater variety of subjects, not all of which were violent or licentious.

37. It should be noted that not all films are a matter of interest here. The so-called "B" films, the tasteless, the tatty, the safe romances without any noticeable points of view and the contrived who-done-its dealing only in stereotypes were being ground out by filmmakers everywhere. However, only the rare exceptions, and there *were* exceptions (which will be addressed in later chapters) made any noise, but they could not, on their own, sustain an industry and they had a minimal effect on film as art.
    The pictures that counted were not always expensive, but they were never "cheap." The thought, the skill, the effort that went into them guaranteed nothing, for creative art is a high-risk endeavor, but they were usually something special. And though it was in the nature of the business that many failed, both critically and financially, it was in the nature of art that even the failures often made important contributions to what Elizabeth Barrett Browning called "Life on a larger scale."

38. I saw a good deal of the film Eisenstein sent back from Mexico. In my opinion it was beautifully-shot material for a documentary, but hardly the makings of a commercial feature film, which he was apparently expected to deliver.

39. In 1942, while viewing some confiscated Japanese films, I was surprised to see actors behaving like everyday human beings, quite unlike the performers in Noh drama which I had believed was the Japanese norm.

40. Today only five major studios are worth a tinker's dam—Paramount, Disney, Warner Brothers, Universal, and Columbia. The latter two are now under foreign control.

41. They often earned more by playing independent houses but the budget remained the same.

42. David Selznick was aware of this shortcoming in some directors and hired production designers to sketch the set-ups for many of his films. In this field, Selznick's great designer, William Cameron Menzies, achieved a worldwide reputation.

43. To apprise my cameraman, Harry Wild, of the lighting style I wanted for *Murder, My Sweet*, I showed him a Daumier chiaroscuro painting. Wild's realization of my request was even more effective than I had hoped for, and played an important part in the development of film noir.

44. In the May 1993 issue of the *Smithsonian*, Israel Shenker writes of Bertrand Russell's reaction to World War I: "To his astonishment he discovered that average men and women were delighted at the prospect of war."

45. For those too young to remember, Lucky Strike cigarettes had been sold in green packs. Apparently, the ingredients of that color were crucial to our cause.

46. A visitor from the Orient recently told me these two films, which, like most of Hollywood's product, have, at the time of this writing, just reached China, are perhaps the most popular films in that country today.

47. One of the country's leading critics, Archer Winston, wrote in the New York Post—"*Crossfire*... a film which is not merely a step forward. It's a step into another world of thinking and doing . . . a film to be seen by all." It also garnered five Oscar nominations; not had for an inexpensive prestige picture.

48. My own version of the hearings, *Odd Man Out*, was published in March of 1996 by the Southern Illinois University Press.

49. *Saturday Review*, May – June 1983.

INDEX

HOLLYWOOD'S GOLDEN AGE

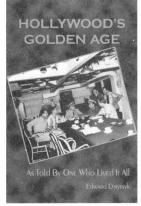

As Told By One Who Lived It All

Edward Dmytryk

RELEASE DATE: July 15, 2003

ISBN: 0-9714570-4-2 $17.95

A legend remembers the good old days of films...

Edward Dmytryk, director of *The Caine Mutiny, Murder, My Sweet, Hitler's Children* and a host of other classic movies, has written a powerful memoir of his early days in Hollywood. From peeking in at the special effects for *The Ten Commandmants*, the original silent film, to his first job as an editor, slowly, patiently splicing film...Dmytryk's brilliantly written and **until now unpublished** look back on old Hollywood is a joy you won't be able to put down.

For fans of old Hollywood—this is the book to savor!

____ YES, please send me ____ copies of *Hollywood's Golden Age* for just $17.95 each.

____ YES, I would like more information about your other publications.

Add $2 postage per book. For non-US orders, please add $5 per book for airmail, in US funds. Payment must accompany all orders. Or buy online with Paypal at bearmanormedia.com.

My check or money order for $_____ is enclosed. Thank you.

NAME _____

ADDRESS_____

CITY/STATE/ZIP _____

EMAIL _____

Checks payable to: BearManor Media * P O Box 750 * Boalsburg, PA 16827
ben@musicdish.com

COMING SUMMER

2004

The Making of
Raintree County
by
Edward Dmytryk

bearmanormedia.com
dmytryk.com